AN
AUTOBIOGR
STUDY

D0662890

By SIGMUND FREUD

Sigmund Freud

AN
AUTOBIOGRAPHICAL
STUDY

TRANSLATED AND EDITED BY

James Strachey

WITH A BIOGRAPHICAL
INTRODUCTION BY

Peter Gay

W·W·NORTON & COMPANY
New York · London

ISBN 0-393-00146-6

W. W. Norton & Company, Inc., is also the publisher of
the Complete Psychological Works of Sigmund Freud.

W. W. Norton & Company, Inc.
500 Fifth Avenue, New York, N.Y. 10110
W. W. Norton & Company Ltd.
10 Coptic Street, London WC1A 1PU

PRINTED IN THE UNITED STATES OF AMERICA

2 3 4 5 6 7 8 9 0

Contents

SIGMUND FREUD: A BRIEF LIFE
by Peter Gay

It was Freud's fate, as he observed not without pride, to "agitate the sleep of mankind." Half a century after his death, it seems clear that he succeeded far better than he expected, though in ways he would not have appreciated. It is commonplace but true that we all speak Freud now, correctly or not. We casually refer to oedipal conflicts and sibling rivalry, narcissism and Freudian slips. But before we can speak that way with authority, we must read his writings attentively. They repay reading, with dividends.

Sigmund Freud was born on May 6, 1856, in the small Moravian town of Freiberg.[1] His father, Jacob Freud, was an impecunious merchant; his mother, Amalia, was handsome, self-assertive, and young—twenty years her husband's junior and his third wife. Jacob Freud had two sons from his first marriage who were about Amalia Freud's age and lived nearby. One of these half brothers had a son, John, who, though Sigmund Freud's nephew, was older than his uncle.

---

[1]His given names were Sigismund Schlomo, but he never used his middle name and, after experimenting with the shorter form for some time, definitively adopted the first name Sigmund—on occasion relapsing into the original formulation—in the early 1870s, when he was a medical student at the University of Vienna. Freiberg, now in Czechoslovakia, bears the Czech name "Pribor "

Freud's family constellation, then, was intricate enough to puzzle the clever and inquisitive youngster. Inquisitiveness, the natural endowment of children, was particularly marked in him. Life would provide ample opportunity to satisfy it.

In 1860, when Freud was almost four, he moved with his family to Vienna, then a magnet for many immigrants. This was the opening phase of the Hapsburg Empire's liberal era. Jews, only recently freed from onerous taxes and humiliating restrictions on their property rights, professional choices, and religious practices, could realistically harbor hopes for economic advancement, political participation, and a measure of social acceptance. This was the time, Freud recalled, when "every industrious Jewish school boy carried a Cabinet Minister's portfolio in his satchel."[2] The young Freud was encouraged to cultivate high ambitions. As his mother's first-born and a family favorite, he secured, once his family could afford it, a room of his own. He showed marked gifts from his first school days, and in his secondary school, or Gymnasium, he was first in his class year after year.

In 1873, at seventeen, Freud entered the University of Vienna. He had planned to study law, but, driven on by what he called his "greed for knowledge," instead matriculated in the faculty of medicine, intending to embark, not on a conventional career as a physician, but on philosophical-scientific investigations that might solve some of the great riddles that fascinated him. He found his work in physiology and neurology so absorbing that he did not take his degree until 1881.

A brilliant researcher, he cultivated the habit of close observation and the congenial stance of scientific skepticism. He was privileged to work under professors with inter-

---

[2] *The Interpretation of Dreams* (1900), *SE* IV, 193.

national reputations, almost all German imports and tough-minded positivists who disdained metaphysical speculations about, let alone pious explanations of, natural phenomena. Even after Freud modified their theories of the mind—in essence barely disguised physiological theories—he recalled his teachers with unfeigned gratitude. The most memorable of them, Ernst Brücke, an illustrious physiologist and a civilized but exacting taskmaster, confirmed Freud's bent as an unbeliever. Freud had grown up with no religious instruction at home, came to Vienna University as an atheist, and left it as an atheist—with persuasive scientific arguments.

In 1882, on Brücke's advice, Freud reluctantly left the laboratory to take a lowly post at the Vienna General Hospital. The reason was romantic: in April, he had met Martha Bernays, a slender, attractive young woman from northern Germany visiting one of his sisters, and fallen passionately in love. He was soon secretly engaged to her, but too poor to establish the respectable bourgeois household that he and his fiancée thought essential. It was not until September 1886, some five months after opening his practice in Vienna, with the aid of wedding gifts and loans from affluent friends, that the couple could marry. Within nine years, they had six children, the last of whom, Anna, grew up to be her father's confidante, secretary, nurse, disciple, and representative, and an eminent psychoanalyst in her own right.

Before his marriage, from October 1885 to February 1886, Freud worked in Paris with the celebrated French neurologist Jean-Martin Charcot, who impressed Freud with his bold advocacy of hypnosis as an instrument for healing medical disorders, and no less bold championship of the thesis (then quite unfashionable) that hysteria is an ailment to which men are susceptible no less than women. Charcot, an unrivaled observer, stimulated Freud's growing interest in the theoretical and therapeutic aspects of mental healing. Nervous ailments became Freud's specialty, and in the 1890s, as he told a friend, psychology became his tyrant. During these years he founded the psychoanalytic theory of mind.

He had intriguing if somewhat peculiar help. In 1887, he had met a nose-and-throat specialist from Berlin, Wilhelm Fliess, and rapidly established an intimate friendship with him. Fliess was the listener the lonely Freud craved: an intellectual gambler shocked at no idea, a propagator of provocative (at times fruitful) theories, an enthusiast who fed Freud ideas on which he could build. For over a decade, Fliess and Freud exchanged confidential letters and technical memoranda, meeting occasionally to explore their subversive notions. And Freud was propelled toward the discovery of psychoanalysis in his practice: his patients proved excellent teachers. He was increasingly specializing in women suffering from hysteria, and, observing their symptoms and listening to their complaints, he found that, though a good listener, he did not listen carefully enough. They had much to tell him.

In 1895, Freud and his fatherly friend Josef Breuer, a thriving, generous internist, published *Studies on Hysteria*, assigning Breuer's former patient "Anna O." pride of place. She had furnished fascinating material for intimate conversations between Breuer and Freud, and was to become, quite against her—and Breuer's—will, the founding patient of psychoanalysis. She demonstrated to Freud's satisfaction that hysteria originates in sexual malfunctioning and that symptoms can be talked away.

The year 1895 was decisive for Freud in other ways. In July, Freud managed to analyze a dream, his own, fully. He would employ this dream, known as "Irma's injection," as a model for psychoanalytic dream interpretation when he published it, some four years later, in his *Interpretation of Dreams*. In the fall, he drafted, but neither completed nor published, what was later called the Project for a Scientific Psychology. It anticipated some of his fundamental theories yet serves as a reminder that Freud had been deeply enmeshed in the traditional physiological interpretation of mental events.

Increasingly Freud was offering psychological explanations for psychological phenomena. In the spring of 1896, he first used the fateful name, "psychoanalysis." Then in October his father died; "the most important event," he recalled a dozen years later, "the most poignant loss, of a man's life."[3] It supplied a powerful impetus toward psychoanalytic theorizing, stirring Freud to his unprecedented self-analysis, more systematic and thoroughgoing than the frankest autobiographer's self-probing. In the next three or four years, as he labored over his "Dream book," new discoveries crowded his days. But first he had to jettison the "seduction theory" he had championed for some time. It held that *every* neurosis results from premature sexual activity, mainly child molestation, in childhood.[4] Once freed from this far-reaching but improbable theory, Freud could appreciate the share of fantasies in mental life, and discover the Oedipus complex, that universal family triangle.

Freud's *Interpretation of Dreams* was published in November 1899.[5] It treated all dreams as wish fulfillments, detailed the mental stratagems that translate their causes

---

[3]Ibid., xxvi.

[4]Freud never claimed that sexual abuse does not exist. He had patients who he knew had not imagined the assaults they reported. All he abandoned when he abandoned the seduction theory was the sweeping claim that *only* the rape of a child, whether a boy or a girl, by a servant, an older sibling, or a classmate, could be the only cause of a neurosis.

[5]The book bears the date of 1900 on the title page and this date is usually given as the date of publication.

into the strange drama the awakening dreamer remembers, and, in the difficult seventh chapter, outlined a comprehensive theory of mind. Its first reception was cool. During six years, only 351 copies were sold; a second edition did not appear until 1909. However, Freud's popularly written *Psychopathology of Everyday Life* of 1901 found a wider audience. Its collection of appealing slips of all sorts made Freud's fundamental point that the mind, however disheveled it might appear, is governed by firm rules. Thus—to give but one typical instance—the presiding officer of the Austrian parliament, facing a disagreeable season, opened it with the formal declaration that it was hereby closed. That "accident" had been prompted by his hidden repugnance for the sessions ahead.

Gradually, though still considered a radical, Freud acquired prestige and supporters. He had quarreled with Fliess in 1900, and, though their correspondence lingered on for some time, the two men never met again. Yet in 1902, after unconscionable delays, apparently generated by anti-Semitism combined with distrust of the maverick innovator, he was finally appointed an associate professor at the University of Vienna. Late that year, Freud and four other Viennese physicians began meeting every Wednesday night in his apartment at Berggasse 19 to discuss psychoanalytic questions; four years after, the group, grown to over a dozen regular participants, employed a paid secretary (Otto Rank) to take minutes and keep records. Finally, in 1908, it was transformed into the Vienna Psychoanalytic Society. At least some medical men (and a few women) were taking Freud's ideas seriously.

In 1905, Freud buttressed the structure of psychoanalytic thought with the second pillar of his theory: the *Three Essays on the Theory of Sexuality.* It outlined perversions and "normal" development from childhood to puberty with a lack of censoriousness and an openness hitherto virtually unknown in medical literature. Again in 1905, Freud brought out his book on jokes and the first of his famous case histories: "Fragment of an Analysis of a Case of Hysteria," nicknamed the "Dora case." He published it to illustrate the uses of dream interpretation in psychoanalysis, and expose his failure to recognize the power of transference in the analytic situation, but its lack of empathy with his embattled teen-age analysand has made it controversial.

In the following decade, Freud enriched the technique of psychoanalysis with three more sophisticated case histories—"Analysis of a Phobia in a Five-Year-Old Boy" ("Little Hans"), "Notes upon a Case of Obsessional Neurosis" ("Rat Man") in 1909, and "Psycho-Analytic Notes on an Autobiographical Account of a Case of Paranoia" ("Schreber Case") in 1911. Despite recent reanalyses, they remain lucid expository models across a wide spectrum of mental ailments. Then, from 1910 on, Freud published pioneering, exceedingly influential papers on technique, to establish psychoanalytic method on sound foundations. Nor did he neglect theory; witness such an important paper as "Formulations on the Two Principles of Mental Functioning" (1911), in which he differentiated between the "primary process," the primitive, unconscious element in the mind, and the "secondary process," largely conscious and controlled.

During these years, Freud also broke out of the circumscribed bounds of clinical and theoretical specialization by publishing papers on religion, literature, sexual mores, biography, sculpture, prehistory, and much else. "Obsessive Actions and Religious Practices" (1907), "Creative Writers and Daydreaming" (1908), " 'Civilized' Sexual Morality and Modern Nervous Illness" (1908), and his widely debated study of the origins of homosexuality, "Leonardo da Vinci and a Memory of His Childhood" (1910), are only samples of his range. Freud took all of culture as his province. He was realizing the program he had outlined for himself in his youth: to solve some of the great riddles of human existence.

Yet Freud also found the decade from 1905 to 1914 agitating with the progress of, and disagreeable splits within, a rapidly emerging international movement—*his* movement. Psychoanalytic politics took center stage. Two principal sources of hope for the future of Freud's ideas, and later of envenomed contention, were the intelligent, Socialist Viennese physician Alfred Adler (1870–1937), and the original, self-willed Swiss psychiatrist Carl G. Jung (1875–1961). Adler had been among Freud's earliest adherents and remained for some years his most prominent Viennese advocate. But as professional interest in psychoanalysis—not all of it benevolent—grew apace, as Freud's upsetting ideas were being explored at psychiatrists' congresses, Freud aspired to enlarge the reach of psychoanalysis beyond its place of origin. Vienna, with its handful of followers, struck him as provincial, unsuitable as headquarters.

The first breakthrough came in 1906, when Jung, then principal psychiatrist at the renowned clinic Burghölzli in Zurich, sent Freud an offprint. Freud responded promptly; a cordial correspondence blossomed, and the friendship was cemented by Jung's visit to Freud in early 1907. Freud was only fifty, vigorous and productive, but he had long brooded on himself as aging and decrepit. He was seeking a successor who would carry the psychoanalytic dispensation to later generations and into a world larger than the Viennese, Jewish ambiance to which psychoanalysis was then confined. Jung, a formidable presence and energetic debater, was an inspired discovery: he was not old, he was not Viennese, he was not Jewish. Jung was prominent in the first international congress of psychoanalysts at Salzburg in the spring of 1908, and was appointed, the following year, editor of a newly founded *Yearbook*. Freud, delighted with Jung, anointed him his son, his crown prince—accolades that Jung welcomed, indeed encouraged. Hence, when the International Psychoanalytic Association was founded in March 1910, in Nürnberg, Jung was Freud's logical, inevitable, choice for president. Freud's Viennese adherents saw their city displaced by Zurich as the center of psychoanalysis, and did not like it. A compromise was hammered out, and for some time peace reigned in the Vienna Psychoanalytic Society. But Adler was developing distinctive psychological ideas, which featured aggressiveness over sexuality, and "organ inferiority" as a dominant cause of neuroses. A split became inevitable, and, in the summer of 1911, Adler and some of his adherents resigned, leaving Freud and the Freudians in control of the Vienna society.

Freud was not without accolades. In September 1909, he had received an honorary doctorate at Clark University in Worcester, Massachusetts, as had Jung. But like Adler, Jung increasingly diverged from Freud's ideas. He had never been easy with the prominence Freud assigned to the sexual drive—libido. By early 1912, these reservations took a personal turn. In response, Ernest Jones, Freud's principal English lieutenant, formed a defensive secret band of like-minded analysts, the Committee. It consisted of himself, Freud, Sandor Ferenczi (a brilliant adherent from Budapest), the witty Viennese lawyer Hanns Sachs, the astute Berlin clinician and theorist Karl Abraham, and Freud's amanuensis, the autodidact Otto Rank. It seemed needed: by late 1912, the correspondence between Jung and Freud had grown acrimonious and in January 1914, Freud terminated his friendship with Jung. A split was only a matter

of time; in the spring of 1914, Jung resigned from his powerful positions in the psychoanalytic movement.

The strains of psychoanalytic politics did not keep Freud
from continuing his explorations of an impressive variety of
topics. In 1913, he published an audacious, highly speculative venture into psychoanalytic prehistory, *Totem and
Taboo,* which specified the moment that savages, in some
dim, remote past, entered culture by murdering their father
and acquiring guilt feelings. Then, in 1914, he published
(anonymously) "The Moses of Michelangelo," uniting his
admiration for Michelangelo's brooding sculpture with his
powers of observation. In the same year, with an unsettling
paper on narcissism, he subverted crucial aspects of psychoanalytic thought by throwing doubts upon his theory of
drives—hitherto divided into erotic and egoistic.

But harrowing events on the world stage shouldered aside
Freud's reassessment of psychoanalytic theory. On June 28,
1914, Austria's Archduke Francis Ferdinand and his consort
were assassinated. Six weeks later, on August 4, Europe was
at war. The first casualty for psychoanalysis was Freud's
eventually best-known case history, "From the History of an
Infantile Neurosis" ("Wolf Man"), written in the fall of
1914, but not published until 1918. Psychoanalytic activity
almost ground to a halt. Many potential patients were at the
front; most psychoanalysts were drafted into the medical
corps; communications between "enemies" like Ernest
Jones and Freud were severely truncated; psychoanalytic
publications almost vanished; and congresses, the lifeblood
of communication, were out of the question. For Freud,
these were anxious times in other ways: all three of his sons
were in the army, two of them almost daily in mortal danger.

Yet the war did not idle Freud's mind. Having too much
time on his hands, he used it to good purpose. Work was a
defense against brooding. Between March and July 1915, he

wrote a dozen fundamental papers on metapsychology—on the unconscious, on repression, on melancholia; but he refused to gather them into the basic textbook he had planned. He published five of the papers between 1915 and 1917, and destroyed the rest. His enigmatic dissatisfaction with them hints at the discontent that had fueled his paper on narcissism. His map of the mind was inadequate to the evidence he had accumulated in his clinical experience. But he still lacked a satisfactory alternative. That would have to wait until after the war.

Another wartime activity, though more successful, gave Freud only modest pleasure: beginning in 1915, he delivered lectures at the university, published as a single volume in 1917 as *Introductory Lectures on Psycho-Analysis*. With the cunning of the born popularizer, Freud opened with a series on ordinary experiences, slips of the tongue, "unmotivated" forgetting, then turned to dreams and concluded with the technical topic, neuroses. Frequently reprinted and widely translated, these *Introductory Lectures* finally secured Freud a wide audience.

The war dragged on. Originally, somewhat to his surprise, an Austrian patriot, Freud wearied of the endless slaughter. He grew appalled at the chauvinism of intellectuals, the callousness of commanders, the stupidity of politicians. He had not yet fully acknowledged the theoretical significance of aggression, even though psychoanalysts had regularly encountered aggressiveness among their patients. But the war, beastly as it was, confirmed the skeptical psychoanalytic appraisal of human nature.

Signs of revived activity came shortly before the end of hostilities. In September 1918, for the first time since 1913, psychoanalysts from Germany and Austria-Hungary met in Budapest. Two months later, the war was over. To the family's immense relief, all of Freud's sons survived it. But the time for worry was far from over. The defeated powers were faced with revolution, drastically transformed from empires into republics, and saddled with stringent, vindictive peace treaties stripping them of territory and resources. Vienna was hungry, cold, desperate; food and fuel shortages produced deadly ailments—tuberculosis and influenza. In this stressful situation, Freud, who wasted no tears on the departed Hapsburg Empire, proved an energetic, imaginative manager. The portrait of Martha Freud shielding Herr Professor from domestic realities needs revision. Freud dispatched precise requests abroad to relatives, friends, associates, specifying what nourishment and clothing his family needed most, and how to send packages safely. Then, in January 1920, postwar misery struck home with deadly force: Freud's beloved second daughter Sophie, married and living in Hamburg, mother of two children, died in the influenza epidemic.

It has been plausibly argued that her death suggested the pessimistic drive theory that Freud now developed. Actually, he had virtually completed *Beyond the Pleasure Principle* (1920), which first announced Freud's theory of the death drive, the year before. Once Freud had adopted this construct, in which the forces of life, Eros, dramatically confront the forces of death, Thanatos, he found himself unable to think any other way. In 1923, in his classic study *The Ego and the Id,* he completed his revisions. He now proposed a "structural theory" of the mind, which visualizes the mind as divided into three distinct yet interacting agencies: the id (the wholly unconscious domain of the mind, consisting of the drives and of material later repressed), the ego (which is partly conscious and contains the defense mechanisms and the capacities to calculate, reason, and plan), and the super-ego (also only partly conscious, which harbors the conscience and, beyond that, unconscious feelings of guilt). This new scheme did not lead Freud to abandon his classic characterization of mental activity—emphasizing the distance of thoughts from awareness—as either conscious, or preconscious, or wholly unconscious. But he now made the decisive point that many of the mental operations of the ego, and of the super-ego as well, are inaccessible to direct introspection.

Meanwhile, the psychoanalytic movement was flourishing. Freud was becoming a household word, though he detested the sensationalized attention the popular press gave him. Better: in 1920, at the first postwar congress at The Hague, former "enemies" met as friends. Freud was accompanied by his daughter Anna, whom he was then analyzing and who joined the Vienna Psychoanalytic Society in 1922. In that year, the analysts convened in Berlin. It was the last congress Freud ever attended. In April 1923, he was operated on for a growth in his palate. While for months his doctors and closest associates pretended that the growth was benign, by September the truth was out: he had cancer. Severe operations followed in the fall. From then on Freud, compelled to wear a prosthesis, was rarely free of discomfort or pain.

But he never stopped working. While he had trouble speaking, he continued to analyze patients, many of them American physicians who came to Vienna as his "pupils" and returned to analyze in New York or Chicago. He continued to revise his theories. From the mid-1920s on, he wrote controversial papers on female sexuality, and, in 1926, *Inhibitions, Symptoms, and Anxiety,* which reversed his earlier thinking on anxiety, now treating it as a danger signal. Moreover, he wrote essays that found a relatively wide public: *The Future of an Illusion,* a convinced atheist's dissection of religion, in 1927, and, in 1930, *Civilization and Its Discontents*, a disillusioned look at modern civilization on the verge of catastrophe.

In 1933, that catastrophe came. On January 30, Hitler was appointed chancellor in Germany, and from then on Austrian Nazis, already active, increasingly intervened in politics. The old guard was disappearing: Karl Abraham had died prematurely in 1925; Sandor Ferenczi followed him in 1933. Freud's closest friends were gone. But Freud was unwilling to leave the Vienna he hated and loved: he was too old, he did not want to desert, and besides, the Nazis would never invade his country. On the morning of March 12, 1938, the Germans proved him wrong. As the Nazis marched in, a jubilant populace greeted them. Spontaneous anti-Semitic outrages surpassed anything Germans had witnessed after five years of Nazi rule. Late in March, Anna was summoned to Gestapo headquarters; while she was released unharmed, the trauma changed Freud's mind: he must emigrate. It took months to satisfy the Nazi government's extortions, but on June 4, Freud left for Paris, welcomed by his former analysand and loving disciple, Princess Marie Bonaparte. On June 6, Freud landed in London, preceded by most of his family, "to die in freedom."

Aged and ill, he kept on working. Freud's last completed book, *Moses and Monotheism*, irritated and dismayed his Jewish readers with its assertion that Moses had been an Egyptian: he ended life as he had lived it—a disturber of the peace. He died bravely on September 23, 1939, asking his physician for a lethal dose of morphine. Freud did not believe in personal immortality, but his work lives on.

About This Book

Freud was no admirer of biographies, not even of biographies with him as its subject. He thought they were bound to be ill-informed, idealizing, even mendacious, productions. Hence, when in 1924 he was asked to participate in a collection of autobiographical statements by prominent physicians, he decided to concentrate on his intellectual development and professional struggles far more than on his inner life. He offered some intimate glimpses, to be sure: his loyalty to his Jewish origins, his brilliance in school, his love for research, his sense of isolation during the years of breaking through to psychoanalysis. There is much to be learned about Freud's ways of thinking in this document. But for the most part, he concentrated on the public rather than the private Freud. One can glean more about his youth, and his deepest feelings, from the autobiographical revelations he scattered across *The Interpretation of Dreams* (1900). The series of four volumes of physicians' autobiographies, titled *Die Medizin der Gegenwart in Selbstdarstellungen* (literally, *The Medicine of the Present Day in Self-Portraits*), was published between 1923 and 1925; the volume in which Freud's "Selbstdarstellung" appeared came out in 1925.

AN
AUTOBIOGRAPHICAL
STUDY

TRANSLATOR'S NOTE

This work appeared originally in 1925 in volume iv of *Die Medizin der Gegenwart in Selbstdarstellungen* (Leipzig: Felix Meiner), a collection of short studies by various members of the medical profession designed (as its title shows) to give a picture of the present state of medicine as revealed in the autobiographies of its leaders. The stress was thus laid by implication upon the professional rather than the personal histories of the contributors; and this limitation applies equally, of course, to the *Autobiographical Study* which is reprinted in the following pages. It would indeed be more accurately described (if the word existed) as an 'auto-ergography'.

The present translation was first published in the United States in 1927 (New York: Brentano) together with another of Professor Freud's writings, *The Problem of Lay-Analyses*, translated by another hand. Both the outer cover and the title-page of that volume, which is now out of print, bore only the title of this latter work, so that the *Autobiographical Study* perhaps attracted less attention than it deserved.

For this new edition the author has made a few alterations and additions to the text and has added some footnotes and a postscript to cover the ten years that have passed since the book was written. The translation has also been revised. A few explanatory footnotes by the translator are distinguished by square brackets.

J. S.

I

Several of the contributors to this series of 'Autobiographical Studies' have begun by expressing their misgivings at the unusual difficulties of the task they have undertaken. The difficulties in my case are, I think, even greater; for I have already more than once published papers upon the same lines as the present one, papers which, from the nature of the subject, have dealt more with personal considerations than is usual or than would otherwise have been necessary.

I gave my first account of the development and subject-matter of psychoanalysis in five lectures which I delivered in 1909 before Clark University at Worcester, Mass., where I had been invited to attend the celebration of the twentieth anniversary of the foundation of that body.[1] Only recently I gave way to the temptation of making a contribution of a similar kind to an American collective publication dealing with the opening years of the twentieth century, since its editors had shown their recognition of the importance of psychoanalysis by allotting a special chapter to it.[2] Between

---

[1] The lectures were first published (in English) in the *American Journal of Psychology* (1910); the original German was issued under the title of *Ueber Psychoanalyse* (Vienna, 1910).

[2] *These Eventful Years* (New York, 1924). My essay, translated by Dr. A. A. Brill, forms chapter lxxiii. of the second volume. [The original German appears in vol. xi. of Freud's *Gesammelte Schriften* (Vienna, 1927).]

these two dates appeared a paper, 'On the History of the Psychoanalytic Movement',[3] which, in fact, contains the essence of all that I can say on the present occasion. Since I must not contradict myself and since I have no wish to repeat myself exactly, I must endeavour to construct a narrative in which subjective and objective attitudes, biographical and historical interests, are combined in a new proportion.

I was born on May 6th, 1856, at Freiberg in Moravia, a small town in what is now Czecho-Slovakia. My parents were Jews, and I have remained a Jew myself. I have reason to believe that my father's family were settled for a long time on the Rhine (at Cologne), that, as a result of a persecution of the Jews during the fourteenth or fifteenth century, they fled eastwards, and that, in the course of the nineteenth century, they migrated back from Lithuania through Galicia into German Austria. When I was a child of four I came to Vienna, and I went through the whole of my education there. At the 'Gymnasium' I was at the top of my class for seven years; I enjoyed special privileges there, and was required to pass scarcely any examinations. Although we lived in very limited circumstances, my father insisted that, in my choice of a profession, I should follow my own inclinations. Neither at that time, nor indeed in my later life, did I feel any particular predilection for the career of a physician. I was moved, rather, by a sort of curiosity, which was, however, directed more towards human concerns than towards natural objects; nor had I grasped the importance of observation as one of the best means of gratifying it. My early familiarity with the Bible story (at a time almost before I had learnt the art of reading) had, as I recognized much later,

---

[3]Published in the *Jahrbuch der Psychoanalyse*, vol. vi., 1914. [English translation in Freud's *Collected Papers*, vol. i.]

an enduring effect upon the direction of my interest. Under the powerful influence of a school friendship with a boy rather my senior who grew up to be a well-known politician I developed a wish to study law like him and to engage in social activities. At the same time, the theories of Darwin, which were then of topical interest, strongly attracted me, for they held out hopes of an extraordinary advance in our understanding of the world; and it was hearing Goethe's beautiful essay on Nature read aloud at a popular lecture by Professor Carl Brühl just before I left school that decided me to become a medical student.

When, in 1873, I first joined the University, I experienced some appreciable disappointments. Above all, I found that I was expected to feel myself inferior and an alien because I was a Jew. I refused absolutely to do the first of these things. I have never been able to see why I should feel ashamed of my descent or, as people were beginning to say, of my race. I put up, without much regret, with my non-acceptance into the community; for it seemed to me that in spite of this exclusion an active fellow-worker could not fail to find some nook or cranny in the framework of humanity. These first impressions at the University, however, had one consequence which was afterwards to prove important; for at an early age I was made familiar with the fate of being in the Opposition and of being put under the ban of the 'compact majority'. The foundations were thus laid for a certain degree of independence of judgment.

I was compelled, moreover, during my first years at the University, to make the discovery that the peculiarities and limitations of my gifts denied me all success in many of the departments of science into which my youthful eagerness had plunged me. Thus I learned the truth of Mephistopheles' warning:

Vergebens, dass ihr ringsum wissenschaftlich schweift, Ein
jeder lernt nur, was er lernen kann.[4]

At length, in Ernst Brücke's physiological laboratory, I
found rest and satisfaction—and men, too, whom I could
respect and take as my models: the great Brücke himself,
and his assistants Sigmund Exner and Ernst von Fleischl-
Marxow. With the last of these, a brilliant man, I was
privileged to be upon terms of friendship. Brücke gave me
a problem to work out in the histology of the nervous system; I succeeded in solving it to his satisfaction and in
carrying the work further on my own account. I worked at
this Institute, with short interruptions, from 1876 to 1882,
and it was generally thought that I was marked out to fill the
next post of Assistant that might fall vacant there. The
various branches of medicine proper, apart from psychiatry,
had no attraction for me. I was decidedly negligent in pursu-
ing my medical studies, and it was not until 1881 that I took
my somewhat belated degree as a Doctor of Medicine.

The turning-point came in 1882, when my teacher, for
whom I felt the highest possible esteem, corrected my father's generous improvidence by strongly advising me, in
view of my bad financial position, to abandon my theoretical
career. I followed his advice, left the physiological laboratory
and entered the General Hospital[5] as an 'Aspirant'. I was
soon afterwards promoted to being a junior resident physician, and worked in various departments of the hospital,
amongst others for more than six months under Meynert,
by whose work and personality I had been greatly struck
while I was still a student.

In a certain sense I nevertheless remained faithful to the

---

[4]['It is in vain that you range around from science to science: each man
learns only what he can learn.'—*Faust,* Part I.]
[5][The principal hospital in Vienna.]

line of work upon which I had originally started. The subject which Brücke had proposed for my investigations had been the spinal cord of one of the lowest of the fishes *(Ammocoetes Petromyzon);* and I now passed on to the human central nervous system. Just at this time Flechsig's discoveries of the non-simultaneity of the formation of the medullary sheaths were throwing a revealing light upon the intricate course of its tracts. The fact that I began by choosing the medulla oblongata as the one and only subject of my work was another sign of the continuity of my development. In complete contrast to the diffuse character of my studies during my earlier years at the University, I was now developing an inclination to concentrate my work exclusively upon a single subject or problem. This inclination has persisted and has since led to my being accused of one-sidedness.

I now became as active a worker in the Institute of Cerebral Anatomy as I had previously been in the physiological one. Some short papers upon the course of the tracts and the nuclear origins in the medulla oblongata date from these hospital years, and my results were regularly noted down by Edinger. One day Meynert, who had given me access to the laboratory even during the times when I was not actually working under him, proposed that I should definitely devote myself to the anatomy of the brain, and promised to hand over his lecturing work to me, as he felt he was too old to manage the newer methods. This I declined, in alarm at the magnitude of the task; it is possible, too, that I had guessed already that this great man was by no means kindly disposed towards me.

From the practical point of view, brain anatomy was certainly no better than physiology, and, with an eye to material considerations, I began to study nervous diseases. There were, at that time, few specialists in that branch of medicine in Vienna, the material for its study was distributed over a number of different departments of the hospital, there was no satisfactory opportunity of learning the subject, and one was forced to be one's own teacher. Even Nothnagel, who had been appointed a short time before, on account of his book upon cerebral localization, did not single out neuropathology from among the other subdivisions of medicine. In the distance glimmered the great name of Charcot; so I formed a plan of first obtaining an appointment as Lecturer on Nervous Diseases in Vienna and of then going to Paris to continue my studies.

In the course of the following years, while I continued to work as a junior physician, I published a number of clinical observations upon organic diseases of the nervous system. I gradually became familiar with the ground; I was able to localize the site of a lesion in the medulla oblongata so accurately that the pathological anatomist had no further information to add; I was the first person in Vienna to send a case for autopsy with a diagnosis of polyneuritis acuta.

The fame of my diagnoses and of their *post-mortem* confirmation brought me an influx of American physicians, to whom I lectured upon the patients in my department in a sort of pidgin-English. I understood nothing about the neuroses. On one occasion I introduced to my audience a neurotic suffering from a persistent headache as a case of chronic localized meningitis; they quite rightly rose in revolt against me, and my premature activities as a teacher came to an end. By way of excuse I may add that this happened at a time when greater authorities than myself in Vienna were in the habit of diagnosing neurasthenia as cerebral tumour.

In the spring of 1885 I was appointed Lecturer on Neuropathology on the ground of my histological and clinical publications. Soon afterwards, as the result of a warm testimonial from Brücke, I was awarded a Travelling Fellowship of considerable value. In the autumn of the same year I made the journey to Paris.

I became a student at the Salpêtrière, but, as one of the crowd of foreign visitors, I had little attention paid me to begin with. One day in my hearing Charcot expressed his regret that since the war he had heard nothing from the German translator of his lectures; he went on to say that he would be glad if someone would undertake to translate the new volume of his lectures into German. I wrote to him and offered to do so; I can still remember a phrase in the letter, to the effect that I suffered only from *'l'aphasie mortrice'* and not from *'l'aphasie sensorielle du français'*. Charcot accepted the offer, I was admitted to the circle of his personal acquaintances, and from that time forward I took a full part in all that went on at the Clinic.

As I write these lines, a number of papers and newspaper articles have reached me from France, which give evidence of a violent objection to the acceptance of psychoanalysis, and which often make the most inaccurate assertions in regard to my relations with the French school. I read, for instance, that I made use of my visit to Paris to familiarize myself with the theories of Pierre Janet and then made off with my booty. I should therefore like to say explicitly that during the whole of my visit to the Salpêtrière Janet's name was never so much as mentioned.

What impressed me most of all while I was with Charcot were his latest investigations upon hysteria, some of which were carried out under my own eyes. He had proved, for instance, the genuineness of hysterical phenomena and their conformity to laws *('introite et hic dii sunt')*, the frequent occurrence of hysteria in men, the production of hysterical paralyses and contractures by hypnotic suggestion and the fact that such artificial products showed, down to their smallest details, the same features as spontaneous attacks,

which were often brought on traumatically. Many of Charcot's demonstrations began by provoking in me and in other
visitors a sense of astonishment and an inclination to scepti-
cism, which we tried to justify by an appeal to one of the
theories of the day. He was always friendly and patient in
dealing with such doubts, but he was also most decided; it
was in one of these discussions that (speaking of theory) he
remarked, *'Ça n'empêche pas d'exister'*, a *mot* which left an
indelible mark upon my mind.

No doubt the whole of what Charcot taught us at that
time does not hold good to-day: some of it has become
doubtful, some has definitely failed to withstand the test of
time. But enough is left over and has found a permanent
place in the storehouse of science. Before leaving Paris I
discussed with the great man a plan for a comparative study
of hysterical and organic paralyses. I wished to establish the
thesis that in hysteria paralyses and anaesthesias of the various parts of the body are demarcated according to the popular idea of their limits and not according to anatomical facts.
He agreed with this view, but it was easy to see that in reality
he took no special interest in penetrating more deeply into
the psychology of the neuroses. When all is said and done,
it was from pathological anatomy that his work had started.

Before I returned to Vienna I stopped for a few weeks in
Berlin, in order to gain a little knowledge of the general
disorders of childhood. Kassowitz, who was at the head of
a public institute in Vienna for the treatment of children's
diseases, had promised to put me in charge of a department
for the nervous diseases of children. In Berlin I was given
assistance and a friendly reception by Baginsky. In the
course of the next few years I published, from the Kassowitz
Institute, several monographs of considerable size on unilat-
eral and bilateral cerebral paralyses in children. And for that
reason, at a later date (in 1897), Nothnagel made me respon-

sible for dealing with the same subject in his great *Hand-buch der allgemeinen und speziellen Therapie.*

In the autumn of 1886 I settled down in Vienna as a physician, and married the girl who had been waiting for me in a distant city for more than four years. I may here go back a little and explain how it was the fault of my *fiancée* that I was not already famous at that early age. A side interest, though it was a deep one, had led me in 1884 to obtain from Merck some of what was then the little-known alkaloid cocaine and to study its physiological action. While I was in the middle of this work, an opportunity arose for making a journey to visit my *fiancée*, from whom I had been parted for two years. I hastily wound up my investigation of cocaine and contented myself in my book on the subject with prophesying that further uses for it would soon be found. I suggested, however, to my friend Königstein, the ophthal-mologist, that he should investigate the question of how far the anaesthetizing properties of cocaine were applicable in diseases of the eye. When I returned from my holiday I found that not he, but another of my friends, Carl Koller (now in New York), whom I had also spoken to about cocaine, had made the decisive experiments upon animals' eyes and had demonstrated them at the Ophthalmological Congress at Heidelberg. Koller is therefore rightly regarded as the discoverer of local anaesthesia by cocaine, which has become so important in minor surgery; but I bore my *fiancée* no grudge for her interruption of my work.

I will now return to the year 1886, the time of my settling down in Vienna as a specialist in nervous diseases. The duty devolved upon me of giving a report before the 'Gesellschaft der Aerzte' [Society of Medicine] upon what I had seen and learnt with Charcot. But I met with a bad reception. Persons of authority, such as the chairman (Bamberger, the physician), declared that what I said was incredible. Meynert urged me to find some cases in Vienna similar to those which I had described and to present them before the Society. I tried to do so; but the senior physicians in whose departments I found any such cases refused to allow me to observe them or to work at them. One of them, an old surgeon, actually broke out with the exclamation: 'But, my dear sir, how can you talk such nonsense? *Hysteron (sic)* means the uterus. So how can a man be hysterical?' I objected in vain that what I wanted was not to have my diagnosis approved, but to have the case put at my disposal. At length, outside the hospital, I came upon a case of classical hysterical hemi-anaesthesia in a man, and demonstrated it before the 'Gesellschaft der Aerzte'. This time I was applauded, but no further interest was taken in me. The impression that the high authorities had rejected my innovations remained unshaken; and, with my hysteria in men and my production of hysterical paralyses by suggestion, I found myself forced into the Opposition. As I was soon afterwards excluded from the laboratory of cerebral anatomy and for a whole session had nowhere to deliver my lectures, I withdrew from academic life and ceased to attend the learned societies. It is a whole generation since I have visited the 'Gesellschaft der Aerzte'.

Anyone who wanted to make a living from the treatment of nervous patients must clearly be able to do something to help them. My therapeutic arsenal contained only two weapons, electrotherapy and hypnotism, for prescribing a visit to a hydropathic establishment after a single consultation was an inadequate source of income. My knowledge of electrotherapy was derived from W. Erb's textbook, which provided detailed instructions for the treatment of all the symptoms of nervous diseases. Unluckily I was soon driven to see that following these instructions was of no help whatever and that what I had taken for an epitome of exact observations was merely the construction of phantasy. The realization that the work of the greatest name in German neuropathology had no more relation to reality than some 'Egyptian' dream-book, such as is sold in cheap bookshops, was painful, but it helped to rid me of another shred of the innocent faith in authority from which I was not yet free. So I put my electrical apparatus aside, even before Möbius had solved the problem by explaining that the successes of electric treatment in nervous disorders (in so far as there were any) were the effect of suggestion on the part of the physician.

With hypnotism the case was better. While I was still a student I had attended a public exhibition given by Hansen the 'magnetist', and had noticed that one of the persons experimented upon had become deathly pale at the onset of cataleptic rigidity and had remained so as long as that condition lasted. This firmly convinced me of the genuineness of the phenomena of hypnosis. Scientific support was soon afterwards given to this view by Heidenhain; but that did not restrain the professors of psychiatry from declaring for a long time to come that hypnotism was not only fraudulent but dangerous and from regarding hypnotists with contempt. In Paris I had seen hypnotism used freely as a method for producing symptoms in patients and then removing them again. And now the news reached us that a school had arisen at Nancy which made an extensive and remarkably successful use of suggestion, with or without hypnosis, for therapeutic purposes. It thus came about, as a matter of course, that in the first years of my activity as a physician my principal instrument of work, apart from haphazard and unsystematic psychotherapeutic methods, was hypnotic suggestion.

This implied, of course, that I abandoned the treatment of organic nervous diseases; but that was of little importance. For on the one hand the prospects in the treatment of such disorders were in any case never promising, while on the other hand, in the private practice of a physician working in a large town, the quantity of such patients was nothing compared to the crowds of neurotics, whose number seemed further multiplied by the manner in which they hurried, with their troubles unsolved, from one physician to another. And apart from this, there was something positively seductive in working with hypnotism. For the first time there was a sense of having overcome one's helplessness; and it was highly flattering to enjoy the reputation of being a miracleworker. It was not until later that I was to discover the drawbacks of the procedure. At the moment there were only two points to complain of: first, that I could not succeed in hypnotizing every patient, and secondly, that I was unable to put individual patients into as deep a state of hypnosis as I should have wished. With the idea of perfecting my hypnotic technique, I made a journey to Nancy in the summer of 1889 and spent several weeks there. I witnessed the moving spectacle of old Liébault working among the poor women and children of the labouring classes, I was a spectator of Bernheim's astonishing experiments upon his hospital patients, and I received the profoundest impression of the possibility that there could be powerful mental processes which nevertheless remained hidden from the consciousness of men. Thinking it would be instructive, I had persuaded one of my patients to follow me to Nancy. She was a very highly gifted hysteric, a woman of good birth, who had been handed over to me because no one knew what to do with her. By hypnotic influence I had made it possible for her to lead a tolerable existence and I was always able to take her out of the misery of her condition. But she always relapsed again after a short time, and in my ignorance I attributed this to the fact that her hypnosis had never reached the stage of somnambulism with amnesia. Bernheim now attempted several times to bring this about, but he too failed. He frankly admitted to me that his great therapeutic successes by means of suggestion were only achieved in his hospital practice and not with his private patients. I had many stimulating conversations with him, and undertook to translate into German his two works upon suggestion and its therapeutic effects.

During the period from 1886 to 1891 I did little scientific work, and published scarcely anything. I was occupied with establishing myself in my new profession and with assuring my own material existence as well as that of a rapidly increasing family. In 1891 there appeared the first of my studies upon the cerebral paralyses of children, which was written in collaboration with my friend and assistant, Dr. Oskar Rie. An invitation which I received in the same year to contribute to an encyclopaedia of medicine led me to investigate the theory of aphasia, which was at that time dominated by the views of Wernicke and Lichtheim, which laid stress exclusively upon localization. The fruit of this enquiry was a small critical and speculative book, *Zur Auffassung der Aphasie*. But I must now show how it happened that scientific research once more became the chief interest of my life.

II

I must supplement what I have just said by explaining that from the very first I made use of hypnosis in another manner, apart from hypnotic suggestion. I used it for questioning the patient upon the origin of his symptom, which in his waking state he could often describe only very imperfectly or not at all. Not only did this method seem more effective than bald suggestive commands or prohibitions, but it also satisfied the curiosity of the physician, who, after all, had a right to learn something of the origin of the phenomenon which he was striving to remove by the monotonous procedure of suggestion.

The manner in which I arrived at this other procedure was as follows. While I was still working in Brücke's laboratory I had made the acquaintance of Dr. Josef Breuer, who was one of the most respected family physicians in Vienna, but who also had a scientific past, since he had produced several works of permanent value upon the physiology of breathing and upon the organ of equilibrium. He was a man of striking intelligence and fourteen years older than myself. Our relations soon became more intimate and he became my friend and helper in my difficult circumstances. We grew accustomed to share all our scientific interests with each other. In this relationship the gain was naturally mine.

The development of psychoanalysis afterwards cost me his friendship. It was not easy for me to pay such a price, but I could not escape it.

Even before I went to Paris, Breuer had told me about a case of hysteria which, between 1880 and 1882, he had treated in a peculiar manner which had allowed him to penetrate deeply into the causation and significance of hysterical symptoms. This was at a time, therefore, when Janet's works still belonged to the future. He repeatedly read me pieces of the case history, and I had an impression that it accomplished more towards an understanding of neuroses than any previous observation. I determined to inform Charcot of these discoveries when I reached Paris, and I actually did so. But the great man showed no interest in my first outline of the subject, so that I never returned to it and allowed it to pass from my mind.

When I was back in Vienna I turned once more to Breuer's observation and made him tell me more about it. The patient had been a young girl of unusual education and gifts, who had fallen ill while she was nursing her father, of whom she was devotedly fond. When Breuer took over her case it presented a variegated picture of paralyses with contractures, inhibitions and states of mental confusion. A chance observation showed her physician that she could be relieved of these clouded states of consciousness if she was induced to express in words the effective phantasy by which she was at the moment dominated. From this discovery, Breuer arrived at a new method of treatment. He put her into deep hypnosis and made her tell him each time what it was that was oppressing her mind. After the attacks of depressive confusion had been overcome in this way, he employed the same procedure for removing her inhibitions and physical disorders. In her waking state the girl could no more describe than other patients how her symptoms had arisen, and she could discover no link between them and any experiences of her life. In hypnosis she immediately revealed the missing connection. It turned out that all her symptoms went back to moving events which she had experienced while nursing her father; that is to say, her symptoms had a meaning and were residues or reminiscences of those emotional situations. It turned out in most instances that there had been some thought or impulse which she had had to suppress while she was by her father's sick-bed, and that, in place of it, as a substitute for it, the symptom had afterwards appeared. But as a rule the symptom was not the precipitate of a single such 'traumatic' scene, but the result of a summation of a number of similar situations. When the patient recalled a situation of this kind in a hallucinatory way under hypnosis and carried through to its conclusion, with a free expression of emotion, the mental act which she had originally suppressed, the symptom was abolished and did not return. By this procedure Breuer succeeded, after long and painful efforts, in relieving his patient of all her symptoms.

The patient had recovered and had remained well and, in fact, had become capable of doing serious work. But over the final stage of this hypnotic treatment there rested a veil of obscurity, which Breuer never raised for me; and I could not understand why he had so long kept secret what seemed to me an invaluable discovery instead of making science the richer by it. The immediate question, however, was whether it was possible to generalize from what he had found in a single case. The state of things which he had discovered seemed to me to be of so fundamental a nature that I could not believe it could fail to be present in any case of hysteria if it had been proved to occur in a single one. But the question could only be decided by experience. I therefore began to repeat Breuer's investigations with my own patients and eventually, especially after my visit to Bernheim in 1889 had taught me the limitations of hypnotic suggestion, I worked at nothing else. After observing for several years that his findings were invariably confirmed in every case of hysteria that was accessible to such treatment, and after having accumulated a considerable amount of material in the shape of observations analogous to his, I proposed to him that we should issue a joint publication. At first he objected vehemently, but in the end he gave way, especially since, in the meantime, Janet's works had anticipated some of his results, such as the tracing back of hysterical symptoms to events in the patient's life, and their removal by means of hypnotic reproduction *in statu nascendi*. In 1893 we issued a preliminary paper, 'On the Psychical Mechanism of Hysterical Phenomena',[1] and in 1895 there followed our book, *Studien über Hysterie.*

If the account I have so far given has led the reader to expect that the *Studien über Hysterie* must, in all the essentials of their material content, be the product of Breuer's mind, that is precisely what I myself have always maintained and what it has been my aim to repeat here. As regards the *theory* put forward in the book, I was partly responsible, but to an extent which it is to-day no longer possible to determine. That theory was in any case unpretentious and hardly went beyond the direct description of the observations. It did not seek to establish the nature of hysteria but merely to throw light upon the origin of its symptoms. Thus it laid stress upon the significance of the life of the emotions and upon the importance of distinguishing between mental acts which are unconscious and those which are conscious (or rather capable of being conscious); it introduced a dynamic factor, by supposing that a symptom arises through the damming-up of an effect, and an economic factor, by regard-

[1][Freud, *Collected Papers*, vol. i.]

ing that same symptom as the product or equivalent of a quantity of energy which would otherwise have been employed in some other way. (This latter process was described as *conversion.*) Breuer spoke of our method as *cathartic;* its therapeutic aim was explained as being to provide that the accumulated effect used for maintaining the symptom, which had got on to the wrong lines and had, as it were, become stuck there, should be directed on to the normal path along which it could obtain discharge (or *abreaction*). The practical results of the cathartic procedure were excellent. Its defects, which became evident later, were those of all forms of hypnotic treatment. There are still a number of psychotherapists who have not gone beyond catharsis as Breuer understood it and who still speak in its favour. Its value as an abridged method of treatment was shown afresh in the hands of Simmel in the treatment of war neuroses in the German army during the Great War. The theory of catharsis had not much to say on the subject of sexuality. In the case histories which I contributed to the *Studien* sexual factors played a certain part, but scarcely more attention was paid to them than to other emotional excitations. Breuer wrote of the girl, who has since become famous as his first patient, that her sexual side was extraordinarily undeveloped. It would have been difficult to guess from the *Studien über Hysterie* what an importance sexuality has in the aetiology of the neuroses.

The stage of development which now followed, the transition from catharsis to psychoanalysis proper, has been described by me several times already in such detail that I shall find it difficult to bring forward any new facts. The event which formed the opening of this period was Breuer's retirement from our common work, so that I became the sole administrator of his legacy. There had been differences of opinion between us at quite an early stage, but they had not been a ground for our separating. In answering the question of when it is that a mental process becomes pathogenic, that is, when it is that it becomes impossible for it to find a normal discharge, Breuer preferred what might be called a physiological theory: he thought that the processes which could not find a normal outcome were such as had originated during unusual, 'hypnoid', mental states. This opened the further question of the origin of these hypnoid states. I, on the other hand, was inclined to suspect the existence of an interplay of forces and the operation of intentions and purposes such as are to be observed in normal life. Thus it was a case of 'Hypnoid Hysteria' versus 'Defence Neurosis'. But such differences as this would scarcely have alienated him from the subject if there had not been other factors at work. One of these was undoubtedly that his work as a physician and family doctor took up much of his time, and that he could not, like me, devote his whole strength to the work of catharsis. Again, he was affected by the reception which our book had received both in Vienna and in Germany. His self-confidence and powers of resistance were not developed so fully as the rest of his mental organization. When, for instance, the *Studien* met with a severe rebuff from Strümpell, I was able to laugh at the lack of comprehension which his criticism showed, but Breuer felt hurt and grew discouraged. But what contributed chiefly to his decision was that my own further work led in a direction to which he found it impossible to reconcile himself.

The theory which we had attempted to construct in the *Studien* remained, as I have said, very incomplete; and in particular we had scarcely touched upon the problem of aetiology, upon the question of the ground in which the pathogenic process takes root. I now learned from my rapidly increasing experience that it was not *any* kind of emotional excitation that was in action behind the phenomena of the neurosis but habitually one of a sexual nature, whether it was a current sexual conflict or the effect of earlier sexual experiences. I was not prepared for this conclusion and my expectations played no part in it, for I had begun my investigation of neurotics quite unsuspectingly. While I was writing my 'History of the Psychoanalytic Movement' in 1914, there recurred to my mind some remarks that had been made to me by Breuer, Charcot, and Chrobak, which might have led me to this discovery earlier. But at the time I heard them I did not understand what these authorities meant; indeed they had told me more than they knew themselves or were prepared to defend. What I heard from them lay dormant and passive within me, until the chance of my cathartic experiments brought it out as an apparently original discovery. Nor was I then aware that in deriving hysteria from sexuality I was going back to the very beginnings of medicine and following up a thought of Plato's. It was not until later that I learnt this from an essay by Havelock Ellis.

Under the influence of my surprising discovery, I now took a momentous step. I went beyond the domain of hysteria and began to investigate the sexual life of the so-called neurasthenics who used to visit me in numbers during my consultation hours. This experiment cost me, it is true, my popularity as a doctor, but it brought me convictions which today, almost thirty years later, have lost none of their force. There was a great deal of equivocation and mystery-making to be overcome, but, once that had been done, it turned out that in all of these patients grave abuses of the sexual function were present. Considering how extremely widespread are these abuses on the one hand and neurasthenia on the other, a frequent coincidence between the two would not have proved much; but there was more in it than that one bald fact. Closer observation suggested to me that it was possible to pick out from the confused jumble of clinical pictures covered by the name of neurasthenia two fundamentally different types, which might appear in any degree of mixture but which were nevertheless to be observed in their pure forms. In the one type the central phenomenon was the anxiety attack with its equivalents, rudimentary forms and chronic surrogate symptoms; I consequently gave it the name of *anxiety neurosis,* and limited the term *neurasthenia* to the other type. Now it was easy to establish the fact that each of these types had a different abnormality of sexual life as its corresponding aetiological factor: in the former, *coitus interruptus,* undischarged excitement and sexual abstinence, and in the latter, excessive masturbation and too numerous nocturnal emissions. In a few specially instructive cases, which had shown a surprising alteration in the clinical picture from one type to the other, it was possible to prove that there had been a corresponding change in the underlying sexual régime. If it was possible to put an end to the abuse and allow its place to be taken by normal sexual activity, a striking improvement in the condition was the reward.

I was thus led into regarding the neuroses as being without exception disturbances of the sexual function, the so-called '*actual*' neuroses being the direct toxic expression of such disturbances and the *psychoneuroses* their mental expression. My medical conscience felt pleased at my having arrived at this conclusion. I hoped that I had filled up a gap in medical science, which, in dealing with a function of such great biological importance, had failed to take into account any injuries beyond those caused by infection or by gross anatomical lesions. The medical aspect of the matter was, moreover, supported by the fact that sexuality was not something purely mental. It had a somatic side as well, and it was possible to assign special chemical processes to it and to attribute sexual excitement to the presence of some particular, though at present unknown, substances. There must also have been some good reason why the true spontaneous neuroses resembled no group of diseases more closely than the phenomena of intoxication and abstinence, which are produced by the administration or privation of certain toxic substances, or than exophthalmic goitre, which is known to depend upon the product of the thyroid gland.

Since that time I have had no opportunity of returning to the investigation of the 'actual' neuroses; nor has this part of my work been continued by anyone else. If I look back to-day at my early findings, they strike me as being the first rough outlines of what is probably a far more complicated subject. But on the whole they seem to me still to hold good. I should have been very glad if I had been able, later on, to make a psychoanalytic examination of some more cases of simple juvenile neurasthenia, but unluckily the occasion did not arise. To avoid misconceptions, I should like to make it clear that I am far from denying the existence of mental conflicts and of neurotic complexes in neurasthenia. All that I am asserting is that the symptoms of these patients are not mentally determined or removable by analysis, but that they must be regarded as direct toxic consequences of disturbed sexual chemical processes.

During the years that followed the publication of the *Studien,* having reached these conclusions upon the part played by sexuality in the aetiology of the neuroses, I read some papers on the subject before various medical societies, but was only met with incredulity and contradiction. Breuer did what he could for some time longer to throw the great weight of his personal influence into the scales in my favour, but he effected nothing and it was easy to see that he too shrank from recognizing the sexual aetiology of neuroses. He might have crushed me or at least disconcerted me by pointing to his own first patient, in whose case sexual factors had ostensibly played no part whatever. But he never did so, and I could not understand why this was until I came to interpret the case correctly and to reconstruct, from some remarks which he had made, the conclusion of his treatment of it. After the work of catharsis had seemed to be completed, the girl had suddenly developed a condition of 'transference love'; he had not connected this with her illness, and had therefore retired in dismay. It was obviously painful to him to be reminded of this apparent *contretemps*. His attitude towards me oscillated for some time between appreciation and bitter criticism; then accidental difficulties arose, as they never fail to do in a strained situation, and we parted.

Another result of my taking up the study of nervous disorders in general was that I altered the technique of catharsis. I abandoned hypnotism and sought to replace it by some other method, because I was anxious not to be restricted to treating hysteriform conditions. Increasing experience had also given rise to two grave doubts in my mind as to the use of hypnotism even as a means to catharsis. The first was that even the most brilliant results were liable to be suddenly wiped away if my personal relation with the patient became disturbed. It was true that they would be re-established if a reconciliation could be effected; but such an occurrence proved that the personal emotional relation between doctor and patient was after all stronger than the whole cathartic process, and it was precisely that factor which escaped every effort at control. And one day I had an experience which showed me in the crudest light what I had long suspected. One of my most acquiescent patients, with whom hypnotism had enabled me to bring about the most marvellous results, and whom I was engaged in relieving of her suffering by tracing back her attacks of pain to their origins, as she woke up on one occasion, threw her arms round my neck. The unexpected entrance of a servant relieved us from a painful discussion, but from that time onwards there was a tacit understanding between us that the hypnotic treatment should be discontinued. I was modest enough not to attribute the event to my own irresistible personal attraction, and I felt that I had now grasped the nature of the mysterious element that was at work behind hypnotism. In order to exclude it, or at all events to isolate it, it was necessary to abandon hypnotism.

But hypnotism had been of immense help in the cathartic treatment, by widening the field of the patient's consciousness and putting within his reach knowledge which he did not possess in his waking life. It seemed no easy task to find a substitute for it. While I was in this perplexity there came to my help the recollection of an experiment which I had often witnessed while I was with Bernheim. When the subject awoke from the state of somnambulism, he seemed to have lost all memory of what had happened while he was in that state. But Bernheim maintained that the memory was present all the same; and if he insisted on the subject remembering, if he asseverated that the subject knew it all and had only to say it, and if at the same time he laid his hand on the subject's forehead, then the forgotten memories used in fact to return, hesitatingly at first, but eventually in a flood and with complete clarity. I determined that I would act in the same way. My patients, I reflected, must in fact 'know' all the things which had hitherto only been made accessible to them in hypnosis; and assurances and encouragement on my part, assisted perhaps by the touch of my hand, would, I thought, have the power of forcing the forgotten facts and connections into consciousness. No doubt this seemed a more laborious process than putting them into hypnosis, but it might prove highly instructive. So I abandoned hypnotism, only retaining my practice of requiring the patient to lie upon a sofa while I sat behind him, seeing him, but not seen myself.

III

My expectations were fulfilled; I was set free from hypnotism. But along with the change in technique the process of catharsis took on a new complexion. Hypnosis had screened from view an interplay of forces which now came in sight and the understanding of which gave a solid foundation to my theory.

How had it come about that the patients had forgotten so many of the facts of their external and internal lives but could nevertheless recollect them if a particular technique was applied? Observation supplied an exhaustive answer to these questions. Everything that had been forgotten had in some way or other been painful; it had been either alarming or disagreeable or shameful by the standards of the subject's personality. The thought arose spontaneously: that was precisely why it had been forgotten, *i.e.* why it had not remained conscious. In order to make it conscious again in spite of this, it was necessary to overcome something that fought against one in the patient; it was necessary to make an expenditure of effort on one's own part in order to compel and subdue it. The amount of effort required of the physician varied in different cases; it increased in direct proportion to the difficulty of what had to be remembered. The expenditure of force on the part of the physician was evidently the measure of a *resistance* on the part of the patient. It was only necessary to translate into words what I myself had observed, and I was in possession of the theory of *repression*.

It was now easy to reconstruct the pathogenic process. Let us keep to a simple example, in which a particular impulsion had arisen in the subject's mind but was opposed by other powerful tendencies. We should have expected the mental *conflict* which now arose to take the following course. The two dynamic quantities—for our present purposes let us call them 'the instinct' and 'the resistance'—would struggle with each other for some time in the fullest light of consciousness, until the instinct was repudiated and the *charge*[1] *of energy* withdrawn from it. This would have been the normal solution. In a neurosis, however (for reasons which were still unknown), the conflict found a different outcome. The ego drew back, as it were, after the first shock of its conflict with the objectionable impulse; it debarred the impulse from access to consciousness and to direct motor discharge, but at the same time the impulse retained its full charge of energy. I named this process *repression;* it was a novelty, and nothing like it had ever before been recognized in mental life. It was obviously a primary mechanism of defence, comparable to an attempt at flight, and was only a forerunner of the later-developed normal condemning judgment. The first act of repression involved further consequences. In the first place the ego was obliged to protect itself against the constant threat of a renewed advance on the part of the repressed impulse by making a permanent

[1][The German word *Besetzung*, here translated 'charge', is applied by Freud to the sum of energy which he supposes to become attached (somewhat upon the analogy of an electric charge) to mental impulses, whether conscious or unconscious, when they are in a condition of activity. The recognized English technical translation of the word is *cathexis.—Trans.*]

expenditure of energy, a *counter-charge* or *anti-cathexis*, and it thus impoverished itself. On the other hand, the repressed impulse, which was now *unconscious*, was able to find means of discharge and of substitutive gratification by circuitous routes and thus to bring the whole purpose of the repression to nothing. In the case of conversion-hysteria the circuitous route led to the nerve supply of the body; the repressed impulse broke its way through at some point or other and produced *symptoms*. The symptoms were thus results of a compromise, for although they were substitutive gratifications they were nevertheless distorted and deflected from their aim owing to the resistance of the ego.

The theory of repression became the foundation-stone of our understanding of the neuroses. A different view had now to be taken of the task of therapy. Its aim was no longer to 'abreact' an affect which had got on to the wrong lines but to uncover repressions and replace them by acts of judgment which might result either in the acceptance or in the rejection of what had formerly been repudiated. I showed my recognition of the new situation by no longer calling my method of investigation and treatment catharsis but *psychoanalysis*.

It is possible to take repression as a centre and to bring all the elements of psychoanalytical theory into relation with it. But before doing so I have a further remark of a polemical nature to make. According to Janet's view a hysterical woman was a wretched creature who, on account of a constitutional weakness, was unable to hold her mental acts together, and it was for that reason that she fell a victim to mental dissociation and to a restriction of the field of her consciousness. The results of psychoanalytical investigations, on the other hand, showed that these phenomena were the result of dynamic factors—of mental conflict and of repression. This distinction seems to me to be far-reaching enough to put an end to the glib repetition of the view that whatever is of value in psychoanalysis is merely borrowed from the ideas of Janet. The reader will have learned from my account that historically psychoanalysis is completely independent of Janet's discoveries, just as in its content it diverges from them and goes far beyond them. Janet's works would never have had the implications which have made psychoanalysis of such importance to the mental sciences and have made it attract such universal interest. I always treated Janet himself with respect, since his discoveries coincided to a considerable extent with those of Breuer, which had been made earlier but were published later than his. But when in the course of time psychoanalysis became a subject of discussion in France, Janet behaved ill, showed ignorance of the facts and used ugly arguments. And finally he revealed himself to my eyes and destroyed the value of his own work by declaring that when he had spoken of 'unconscious' mental acts he had meant nothing by the phrase—it had been no more than a *façon de parler.*

But the study of pathogenic repressions and of other phenomena which have still to be mentioned compelled psychoanalysis to take the concept of the 'unconscious' seriously. Psychoanalysis regarded everything mental as being in the first instance unconscious; the further quality of 'consciousness' might also be present, or again it might be absent. This of course provoked a denial from the philosophers, for whom 'conscious' and 'mental' were identical, and who protested that they could not conceive of such a monstrosity as the 'unconscious mental'. There was no help for it, however, and this idiosyncrasy of the philosophers could only be disregarded with a shrug. Experience (gained from pathological material, of which the philosophers were ignorant) of the frequency and power of impulses of which one knew nothing directly and whose existence had to be inferred like some fact in the external world, left no alternative open. It could be pointed out, incidentally, that this was only treating one's own mental life as one had always treated other people's. One did not hesitate to ascribe mental processes to other people, although one had no immediate consciousness of them and could only infer them from their words and actions. But what held good for other people must be applicable to oneself. Anyone who tried to push the argument further and to conclude from it that one's own hidden processes belonged actually to a second *consciousness* would be faced with the concept of a consciousness of which one knew nothing, of an 'unconscious consciousness'—and this would scarcely be preferable to the assumption of an 'unconscious mental'. If, on the other hand, one declared, like some other philosophers, that one was prepared to take pathological phenomena into account, but that the processes underlying them ought not to be described as mental but as 'psychoid', the difference of opinion would degenerate into an unfruitful dispute about words, though even so expediency would decide in favour of keeping the expression 'unconscious mental'. The further question as to the ultimate nature of this unconscious is no wiser or more profitable than the older one as to the nature of the conscious.

It would be more difficult to explain concisely how it came about that psychoanalysis made a further distinction in the unconscious, and separated it into a *preconscious* and an unconscious proper. It will be sufficient to say that it appeared a legitimate course to supplement the theories which were a direct expression of experience by hypotheses which were designed to facilitate the handling of the material and related to matters which could not be a subject of immediate observation. The very same procedure is adopted by the older sciences. The subdivision of the unconscious is part of an attempt to picture the apparatus of the mind as being built up of a number of *functional systems* whose interrelations may be expressed in spatial terms, without reference, of course, to the actual anatomy of the brain. (I have described this as the *topographical* method of approach.) Such ideas as these are part of a speculative superstructure of psychoanalysis, any portion of which can be abandoned or changed without loss or regret the moment its inadequacy has been proved. But there is still plenty to be described that lies closer to actual experience.

I have already mentioned that my investigation of the precipitating and underlying causes of the neuroses led me more and more frequently to conflicts between the subject's sexual impulses and his resistances to sexuality. In my search for the pathogenic situations in which the repressions of sexuality had set in and in which the symptoms, as substitutes for what was repressed, had had their origin, I was carried further and further back into the patient's life and ended by reaching the first years of his childhood. What poets and students of human nature had always asserted turned out to be true: the impressions of that remote period of life, though they were for the most part buried in amnesia, left ineradicable traces upon the individual's growth and in particular laid the foundations of any nervous disorder that was to follow. But since these experiences of childhood were always concerned with sexual excitations and the reaction against them, I found myself faced by the fact of infantile sexuality—once again a novelty and a contradiction of one of the strongest of human prejudices. Childhood was looked upon as 'innocent' and free from the lusts of sex, and the fight with the demon of 'sensuality' was not thought to begin until the troubled age of puberty. Such occasional sexual activities as it had been impossible to overlook in children were put down as signs of degeneracy and premature depravity or as a curious freak of nature. Few of the findings of psychoanalysis have met with such universal contradiction or have aroused such an outburst of indignation as the assertion that the sexual function starts at the beginning of life and reveals its presence by important signs even in childhood. And yet no other findings of analysis can be demonstrated so easily and so completely.

Before going further into the question of infantile sexuality I must mention an error into which I fell for a while and which might well have had fatal consequences for the whole of my work. Under the pressure of the technical procedure which I used at that time, the majority of my patients reproduced from their childhood scenes in which they were sexually seduced by some grown-up person. With female patients the part of seducer was almost always assigned to their father. I believed these stories, and consequently supposed that I had discovered the roots of the subsequent neurosis in these experiences of sexual seduction in childhood. My confidence was strengthened by a few cases in which relations of this kind with a father, uncle, or elder brother had continued up to an age at which memory was to be trusted. If the reader feels inclined to shake his head at my credulity, I cannot altogether blame him; though I may plead that this was at a time when I was intentionally keeping my critical faculty in abeyance so as to preserve an unprejudiced and receptive attitude towards the many novelties which were coming to my notice every day. When, however, I was at last obliged to recognize that these scenes of seduction had never taken place, and that they were only phantasies which my patients had made up or which I myself had perhaps forced upon them, I was for some time completely at a loss. My confidence alike in my technique and in its results suffered a severe blow; it could not be disputed that I had arrived at these scenes by a technical method which I considered correct, and their subject-matter was unquestionably related to the symptoms from which my investigation had started. When I had pulled myself together, I was able to draw the right conclusions from my discovery: namely, that the neurotic symptoms were not related directly to actual events but to phantasies embodying wishes, and that as far as the neurosis was concerned psychical reality was of more importance than material reality. I do not believe even now that I forced the seduction-phantasies upon my patients, that I 'suggested' them. I had in fact stumbled for the first time upon the *Oedipus complex*, which was later to assume such an overwhelming importance, but which I did not recognize as yet in its disguise of phantasy. Moreover, seduction during childhood retained a certain share, though a humbler one, in the aetiology of neuroses. But the seducers turned out as a rule to have been older children.

It will be seen, then, that my mistake was of the same kind as would be made by someone who believed that the legendary story of the early kings of Rome (as told by Livy) was historical truth instead of what it is in fact—a reaction against the memory of times and circumstances that were insignificant and occasionally, perhaps, inglorious. When the mistake had been cleared up, the path to the study of the sexual life of children lay open. It thus became possible to apply psychoanalysis to another field of science and to use its data as a means of discovering a new piece of biological knowledge.

The sexual function, as I found, is in existence from the very beginning of the individual's life, though at first it is assimilated to the other vital functions and does not become independent of them until later; it has to pass through a long and complicated process of development before it becomes what we are familiar with as the normal sexual life of the

adult. It begins by manifesting itself in the activity of a
whole number of *component instincts*. These are dependent
upon *erotogenic zones* in the body; some of them make their
appearance in pairs of opposite impulses (such as sadism and
masochism or the impulses to look and to be looked at); they
operate independently of one another in their search for
pleasure, and they find their object for the most part in the
subject's own body. Thus to begin with they are non-central-
ized and predominantly *auto-erotic*. Later they begin to be
co-ordinated; a first stage of organization is reached under
the dominance of the *oral* components, and *anal-sadistic*
stage follows, and it is only after the third stage has at last
been reached that the primacy of the *genitals* is established
and that the sexual function begins to serve the ends of
reproduction. In the course of this process of development
a number of elements of the various component instincts
turn out to be unserviceable for this last end and are therefore left on one side or turned to other uses, while others are
diverted from their aims and carried over into the genital
organization. I gave the name of *libido* to the energy of the
sexual instincts and to that form of energy alone. I was next
driven to suppose that the libido does not always pass
through its prescribed course of development smoothly. As
a result either of the excessive strength of certain of the
components or of experiences involving premature gratification, *fixations* of the libido may occur at various points in
the course of its development. If subsequently a repression
takes place, the libido flows back to these points (a process
described as *regression*), and it is from them that the energy
breaks through in the form of a symptom. Later on it further
became clear that the localization of the point of fixation is
what determines the *choice of neurosis,* that is, the form in
which the subsequent illness makes its appearance.

The process of arriving at an *object,* which plays such an

important part in mental life, takes place alongside of the organization of the libido. After the stage of *auto-erotism*, the first love-object in the case of both sexes is the mother; and it seems probable that to begin with the child does not distinguish its mother's organ of nutrition from its own body. Later, but still in the first years of infancy, the relation known as the Oedipus complex becomes established: boys concentrate their sexual wishes upon their mother and develop hostile impulses against their father as being a rival, while girls adopt an analogous attitude.[2] All of the different variations and consequences of the Oedipus complex are important; and in particular the innately bisexual constitution of human beings makes itself felt and increases the number of simultaneously active tendencies. Children do not become clear for quite a long time upon the differences between the sexes; and during this period of *sexual enquiry* they produce typical *sexual theories* which, since they are limited by the incompleteness of their authors' own physical development, are a mixture of truth and error and fail to solve the problems of sexual life (the riddle of the Sphinx— the question of where babies come from). We see, then, that a child's first object-choice is an *incestuous* one. The whole course of development that I have described is run through rapidly. For the most remarkable feature of the sexual life

---

[2](Additional note, 1935.) The information about infantile sexuality was obtained from the study of men and the theory deduced from it was concerned with male children. It was natural enough to expect to find a complete parallel between the two sexes; but this turned out not to hold. Further investigations and reflections revealed profound differences between the sexual development of men and women. The first sexual object of a baby girl (just as of a baby boy) is her mother; and before a woman can reach the end of her normal development she has to change not only her sexual object but also her predominant genital zone. From this circumstance difficulties arise and possibilities of inhibition which are not present in the case of men.

of man is that it comes on in two waves, with an interval between them. It reaches a first maximum in the fourth or fifth year of a child's life. But this early growth of sexuality is nipped in the bud; the sexual impulses which have shown such liveliness are overcome by repression, and a *period of latency* follows, which lasts until puberty and during which the *reaction-formations* of morality, shame, and disgust are built up.[3] Of all living creatures man alone seems to show this double onset of sexual growth, and it may perhaps be the biological determinant of his predisposition to neuroses. At puberty the impulses and object-relations of a child's early years become re-animated, and amongst them the emotional ties of his Oedipus complex. The sexual life of puberty is a struggle between the impulses of early years and the inhibitions of the latency period. Before this, and while the child is at the highest point of its infantile sexual development, a genital organization of a sort is established; but only the male genitals play a part in it, and the female ones remain undiscovered. (I have described this as the period of *phallic* primacy.) At this stage the contrast between the sexes is not stated in terms of 'male' or 'female' but of 'possessing a penis' or 'castrated'. The *castration complex* which arises in this connection is of the profoundest importance in the formation alike of character and of neuroses.

In order to make this condensed account of my discoveries upon the sexual life of man more intelligible, I have brought together conclusions which I reached at different dates and incorporated by way of supplement or correction in the successive editions of my *Three Contributions to the*

---

[3](Additional note, 1935.) The period of latency is a physiological phenomenon. It can, however, only give rise to a complete interruption of sexual life in cultural organizations which have made the suppression of infantile sexuality a part of their system. This is not the case with the majority of primitive peoples.

Theory of Sexuality. [4] I hope it will have been easy to gather the nature of my extension (on which so much stress has been laid and which has excited so much opposition) of the concept of sexuality. That extension is of a twofold kind. In the first place sexuality is divorced from its too close connection with the genitals and is regarded as a more comprehensive bodily function, having pleasure as its goal and only secondarily coming to serve the ends of reproduction. In the second place the sexual impulses are regarded as including all of those merely affectionate and friendly impulses to which usage applies the exceedingly ambiguous word 'love'. I do not, however, consider that these extensions are innovations but rather restorations: they signify the removal of inexpedient limitations of the concept into which we had allowed ourselves to be led.

The detaching of sexuality from the genitals has the advantage of allowing us to bring the sexual activities of children and of perverts into the same scope as those of normal adults. The former have hitherto been entirely neglected and though the latter have been recognized it has been with moral indignation and without understanding. Looked at from the psychoanalytic standpoint, even the most eccentric and repellent perversions are explicable as manifestations of component instincts of sexuality which have freed themselves from the primacy of the genitals and are going in pursuit of pleasure on their own account as they did in the very early days of the libido's development. The most important of these perversions, homosexuality, scarcely deserves the name. It can be traced back to the constitutional bisexuality of all human beings and to the after-effects of the phallic primacy. Psychoanalysis enables us to point to some

---

[4][First German edition, under the title of *Drei Abhandlungen zur Sexualtheorie*, Vienna, 1905.]

trace or other of a homosexual object-choice in everyone. If I have described children as 'polymorphously perverse', I was only using a terminology that was generally current; no moral judgment was implied by the phrase. Psychoanalysis has no concern whatever with such judgements of value.

The second of my alleged extensions of the concept of sexuality finds its justification in the fact revealed by psychoanalytic investigation that all of these affectionate impulses were originally of a completely sexual nature but have become *inhibited in their aim* or *sublimated*. The manner in which the sexual instincts can thus be influenced and diverted enables them to be employed for cultural activities of every kind, to which indeed they bring the most important contributions.

My surprising discoveries as to the sexuality of children were made in the first instance through the analysis of adults. But later (from about 1908 onwards) it became possible to confirm them in the most satisfactory way and in every detail by direct observations upon children. Indeed, it is so easy to convince oneself of the regular sexual activities of children that one cannot help asking in astonishment how the human race can have succeeded in overlooking the facts and in maintaining for so long the agreeable legend of the asexuality of childhood. This surprising circumstance must be connected with the amnesia which, with the majority of adults, hides their own infancy.

IV

The theories of resistance and of repression, of the unconscious, of the aetiological significance of sexual life and of the importance of infantile experiences—these form the principal constituents of the theoretical structure of psychoanalysis. In these pages, unfortunately, I have been able to describe only the separate elements and not their interconnections and their bearing upon one another. But I am obliged now to turn to the alterations which gradually took place in the technique of the analytic method.

The means which I first adopted for overcoming the patient's resistance, by pressing and encouraging him, had been indispensable for the purpose of giving me a first general survey of what was to be expected. But in the long run it proved to be too much of a strain upon both sides, and further it seemed open to certain obvious criticisms. It therefore gave place to another method which was in one sense its opposite. Instead of urging the patient to say something upon some particular subject, I now asked him to abandon himself to a process of *free association, i.e.* to say whatever came into his head, while ceasing to give any conscious direction to his thoughts. It was essential, however, that he should bind himself to report literally everything that occurred to his self-perception and not to give way to critical objections which sought to put certain associations on one side on the ground that they were not sufficiently important or that they were irrelevant or that they were altogether meaningless. There was no necessity to repeat explicitly the insistence upon the need for candour on the patient's part in reporting his thoughts, for it was the precondition of the whole analytic treatment.

It may seem surprising that this method of free association, carried out subject to the observation of *the fundamental rule of psychoanalysis*, should have achieved what was expected of it, namely the bringing into consciousness of the repressed material which was held back by resistances. We must, however, bear in mind that free association is not really free. The patient remains under the influence of the analytic situation even though he is not directing his mental activities on to a particular subject. We shall be justified in assuming that nothing will occur to him that has not some reference to that situation. His resistance against reproducing the repressed material will now be expressed in two ways. Firstly it will be shown by critical objections; and it was to deal with these that the fundamental rule of psychoanalysis was invented. But if the patient observes that rule and so overcomes his reticences, the resistance will find another means of expression. It will so arrange it that the repressed material itself will never occur to the patient but only something which approximates to it in an allusive way; and the greater the resistance, the more remote will be the substitutive association which the patient has to report from the actual idea that the analyst is in search of. The analyst, who listens composedly but without any constrained effort to the stream of associations and who, from his experience, has a general notion of what to expect, can make use of the material brought to light by the patient according to two possibilities. If the resistance is slight he will be able from the patient's allusions to infer the unconscious material itself; or if the resistance is stronger he will be able to recognize its character from the associations, as they seem to become more remote from the subject, and will explain it to the patient. Uncovering the resistance, however, is the first step towards overcoming it. Thus the work of analysis involves an *art of interpretation*, the successful handling of which may require tact and practice but which is not hard to acquire. But it is not only in the saving of labour that the method of free association has an advantage over the earlier method. It exposes the patient to the least possible amount of compulsion, it never allows of contact being lost with the actual current situation, it guarantees to a great extent that no factor in the structure of the neurosis will be overlooked and that nothing will be introduced into it by the expectations of the analyst. It is left to the patient in all essentials to determine the course of the analysis and the arrangement of the material; any systematic handling of particular symptoms or complexes thus becomes impossible. In complete contrast to what happened with hypnotism and with the urging method, interrelated material makes its appearance at different times and at different points in the treatment. To a spectator, therefore—though in fact there can be none—an analytic treatment would seem completely obscure.

Another advantage of the method is that it need never break down. It must theoretically always be possible to have an association, provided that no conditions are made as to its character. Yet there is one case in which in fact a breakdown occurs with absolute regularity; from its very uniqueness, however, this case too can be interpreted.

I now come to the description of a factor which adds an essential feature to my picture of analysis and which can claim, alike technically and theoretically, to be regarded as of the first importance. In every analytic treatment there arises, without the physician's agency, an intense emotional relationship between the patient and the analyst which is not to be accounted for by the actual situation. It can be of a positive or of a negative character and can vary between the extremes of a passionate, completely sensual love and the unbridled expression of an embittered defiance and hatred. This *transference*—to give it its shortened name—soon replaces in the patient's mind the desire to be cured, and, so long as it is affectionate and moderate, becomes the agent of the physician's influence and neither more nor less than the mainspring of the joint work of analysis. Later on, when it has become passionate or has been converted into hostility, it becomes the principal tool of the resistance. It may then happen that it will paralyse the patient's powers of associating and endanger the success of the treatment. Yet it would be senseless to try to evade it; for an analysis without transference is an impossibility. It must not be supposed, however, that transference is created by analysis and does not occur apart from it. Transference is merely uncovered and isolated by analysis. It is a universal phenomenon of the human mind, it decides the success of all medical influence, and in fact dominates the whole of each person's relations to his human environment. We can easily recognize it as the same dynamic factor that the hypnotists have named 'suggestibility', which is the agent of hypnotic *rapport* and whose incalculable behaviour led to such difficulties with the cathartic method. When there is no inclination to a transference of emotion such as this, or when it has become entirely negative, as happens in dementia praecox or paranoia, then there is also no possibility of influencing the patient by psychological means.

It is perfectly true that psychoanalysis, like other psychotherapeutic methods, employs the instrument of suggestion (or transference). But the difference is this: that in analysis it is not allowed to play the decisive part in determining the therapeutic results. It is used instead to induce the patient to perform a piece of mental work—the overcoming of his transference-resistances—which involves a permanent alteration in his mental economy. The transference is made conscious to the patient by the analyst, and it is resolved by convincing him that in his transference-attitude he is *re-experiencing* emotional relations which had their origin in his earliest object-attachments during the repressed period of his childhood. In this way the transference is changed from the strongest weapon of the resistance into the best instrument of the analytic treatment. Nevertheless its handling remains the most difficult as well as the most important part of the technique of analysis.

With the help of the method of free association and of the closely related art of interpretation, psychoanalysis succeeded in achieving one thing which appeared to be of no practical importance but which in fact necessarily led to a fresh attitude and a fresh scale of values in scientific thought. It became possible to prove that dreams have a meaning and to discover it. In classical antiquity great importance was attached to dreams as foretelling the future; but modern science would have nothing to do with them, it handed them over to superstition, declaring them to be purely 'somatic' processes—a kind of spasm occurring in a mind that is otherwise asleep. It seemed quite inconceivable that anyone who had done serious scientific work could make his appearance as an 'interpreter of dreams'. But by disregarding the excommunication pronounced upon dreams, by treating them as unexplained neurotic symptoms, as delusional or obsessional ideas, by neglecting their apparent content and by making their separate component images into subjects for free association, psychoanalysis arrived at a different conclusion. The numerous associations produced by the dreamer led to the discovery of a mental structure which could no longer be described as absurd or confused, which was on an equality with any other product of the mind, and of which the *manifest* dream was no more than a distorted, abbreviated, and misunderstood translation, and usually a translation into visual images. These *latent dream-thoughts* contained the meaning of the dream, while its manifest content was simply a make-believe, a façade, which could serve as a starting-point for the associations but not for the interpretation.

There were now a whole series of questions to be answered, among the most important of them being whether there was a motive for the formation of dreams, under what conditions it took place, by what methods the dream-thoughts (which are invariably full of sense) become converted into the dream (which is often senseless), and others besides. I attempted to solve all of these problems in *The Interpretation of Dreams*,[1] which I published in the year 1900. I can only find space here for the briefest abstract of my investigation. When the latent dream-thoughts that are revealed by the analysis of a dream are examined, one of them is found to stand out from among the rest, which are intelligible and well known to the dreamer. These latter thoughts are residues of waking life (the *day's residues*, as they are called technically); but the isolated thought is found to be an impulse in the form of a wish, often of a very repellent kind, which is foreign to the waking life of the dreamer and is consequently disavowed by him with surprise or indignation. This impulse is the actual constructor of the dream: it provides the energy for its production and makes use of the day's residues as material; the dream which thus

---

[1] [*Die Traumdeutung*, Vienna, 1900.]

originates represents a situation in which the impulse is satisfied, it is the fulfilment of the wish which the impulse contains. It would not be possible for this process to take place without being favoured by the presence of something in the nature of a state of sleep. The necessary mental pre-condition of sleep is the concentration of the ego upon the wish to sleep and the withdrawal of psychical energy from all the interests of life; since at the same time all the paths of approach to motility are blocked, the ego is also able to reduce the expenditure of energy by which at other times it maintains the repressions. The unconscious impulse makes use of this nocturnal relaxation of repression in order to push its way into consciousness with the dream. But the repressive resistance of the ego is not abolished in sleep but merely reduced. Some of it remains in the shape of a *censorship of dreams* and forbids the unconscious impulse to express itself in the forms which it would properly assume. In consequence of the severity of the censorship of dreams, the latent dream-thoughts are obliged to submit to being altered and softened so as to make the forbidden meaning of the dream unrecognizable. This is the explanation of *dream-distortion,* which accounts for the most striking characteristic of the manifest dream. We are therefore justified in asserting that *a dream is the (disguised) fulfilment of a (repressed) wish.* It will now be seen that dreams are constructed like a neurotic symptom: they are compromises between the demands of a repressed impulse and the resistance of a censoring force in the ego. Since they have a similar origin they are equally unintelligible and stand in equal need of interpretation.

There is no difficulty in discovering the general function of dreaming. It serves the purpose of warding off, by a kind of soothing action, external or internal stimuli which would tend to arouse the sleeper, and thus of securing sleep against interruption. External stimuli are warded off by being given a new interpretation and by being woven into some harmless situation; internal stimuli, caused by the pressure of instincts, are given free play by the sleeper and allowed to find satisfaction in the formation of dreams, so long as the latent dream-thoughts submit to the control of the censorship. But if they threaten to break free and the meaning of the dream becomes too plain, the sleeper cuts short the dream and awakens in terror. (Dreams of this class are known as *anxiety-dreams.*) A similar failure in the function of dreaming occurs if an external stimulus becomes too strong to be warded off. (This is the class of *arousal-dreams.*) I have given the name of *dream-work* to the process which, with the cooperation of the censorship, converts the latent thoughts into the manifest content of the dream. It consists of a peculiar way of treating the preconscious material of thought, so that its component parts become *condensed,* its mental emphasis becomes *displaced,* and the whole of it is translated into visual images or *dramatized,* and filled out by a deceptive *secondary elaboration.* The dream-work is an excellent example of the processes occurring in the deeper, unconscious layers of the mind, which differ considerably from the familiar normal processes of thought. It also displays a number of archaic characteristics, such as the use of a *symbolism* (in this case of a predominantly sexual kind) which it has since also been possible to discover in other spheres of mental activity.

We have explained that the unconscious impulse which causes the dream connects itself with part of the day's residues, with some unexhausted interest of waking life; this lends the dream which is thus brought into being a double value for the work of analysis. It is true that on the one hand a dream that has been analysed reveals itself as the fulfilment of a repressed wish; but on the other hand it will be a continuation of some preconscious activity of the day before and will contain subject-matter of some kind or other, whether it gives expression to a determination, a warning, a reflection, or once more to the fulfilment of a wish. Analysis exploits the dream in both directions, as a means of obtaining knowledge alike of the patient's conscious and of his unconscious processes. It also profits from the fact that dreams have access to the forgotten material of childhood, and so it happens that infantile amnesia is for the most part overcome in connection with the interpretation of dreams. In this respect dreams achieve a part of what was previously the task of hypnotism. On the other hand, I have never maintained the assertion which has so often been ascribed to me that dream-interpretation shows that all dreams have a sexual content or are derived from sexual motive forces. It is easy to see that hunger, thirst, or the need to excrete, can produce dreams of satisfaction just as well as any repressed sexual or egoistic impulse. The case of young children affords us a convenient test of the validity of our theory of dreams. In them the various psychical systems are not yet sharply divided and the repressions have not yet grown deep, so that we often come upon dreams which are nothing more than undisguised fulfilments of impulses left over from waking life. Under the influence of imperative needs, adults may also produce dreams of this infantile type.[2]

In the same way that psychoanalysis makes use of dream-interpretation, it also profits by the study of the numerous little slips and mistakes which people make—symptomatic

---

[2](Additional note, 1935.) When it is considered how frequently the function of dreaming miscarries, the dream may aptly be characterized as an *attempt* at the fulfilment of a wish. Aristotle's old definition of the dream as mental life during sleep still holds good. There was a reason for my choosing as the title of my book not *The Dream* but *The Interpretation of Dreams.*

actions, as they are called. I investigated this subject in a series of papers which were published for the first time in book form in 1904 under the title of *The Psychopathology of Everyday Life*.[3] In this widely circulated work I have pointed out that these phenomena are not accidental, that they require more than physiological explanations, that they have a meaning and can be interpreted, and that one is justified in inferring from them the presence of restrained or repressed impulses and intentions. But what constitutes the enormous importance of dream-interpretation, as well as of this latter study, is not the assistance they give to the work of analysis but another of their attributes. Previously psychoanalysis had only been concerned with solving pathological phenomena and in order to explain them it had often been driven into making assumptions whose comprehensiveness was out of all proportion to the importance of the actual material under consideration. But when it came to dreams, it was no longer dealing with a pathological symptom, but with a phenomenon of normal mental life which might occur in any healthy person. If dreams turned out to be constructed like symptoms, if their explanation required the same assumptions—the repression of impulses, substitute-formation, compromise-formation, the dividing of the conscious and the unconscious into various psychical systems—then psychoanalysis was no longer a subsidiary science in the field of psychopathology, it was rather the foundation for a new and deeper science of the mind which would be equally indispensable for the understanding of the normal. Its postulates and findings could be carried over to other regions of mental happening; a path lay open to it that led far afield, into spheres of universal interest.

---

[3][*Zur Psychopathologie des Alltagslebens*, Berlin, 1904.]

V

I must interrupt my account of the internal growth of psychoanalysis and turn to its external history. What I have so far described of its discoveries has related for the most part to the results of my own work; but I have filled in my story with material from later dates and have not distinguished between my own contributions and those of my pupils and followers.

For more than ten years after my separation from Breuer I had no followers. I was completely isolated. In Vienna I was shunned; abroad no notice was taken of me. My *Interpretation of Dreams*, published in 1900, was scarcely reviewed in the technical journals. In my paper 'On the History of the Psycho-Analytic Movement' I mentioned as an instance of the attitude adopted by psychiatric circles in Vienna a conversation with an assistant at the Clinic, who had written a book against my theories but had never read by *Interpretation of Dreams*. He had been told at the Clinic that it was not worth while. The man in question, who has since become a professor, has gone so far as to repudiate my report of the conversation and to throw doubts in general upon the accuracy of my recollection. I can only say that I stand by every word of the account I then gave.

As soon as I realized the inevitable nature of what I had

come up against, my sensitiveness greatly diminished. Moreover my isolation gradually came to an end. To begin with, a small circle of pupils gathered round me in Vienna; and then, after 1906, came the news that the psychiatrists at Zurich, E. Bleuler, his assistant C. G. Jung, and others, were taking a lively interest in psychoanalysis. We got into personal touch with one another, and at Easter 1908 the friends of the young science met at Salzburg, agreed upon the regular repetition of similar informal congresses and arranged for the publication of a journal which was edited by Jung and was given the title of *Jahrbuch für psychopathologische und psychoanalytische Forschungen*. It was brought out under the direction of Bleuler and myself and ceased publication at the beginning of the Great War. At the same time that the Swiss psychiatrists joined the movement, interest in psychoanalysis began to be aroused all over Germany; it became the subject of a large number of written comments as well as of lively discussions at scientific congresses. But its reception was nowhere friendly or even benevolently impartial. After the briefest acquaintance with psychoanalysis German science was united in rejecting it.

Even to-day it is of course impossible for me to foresee the final judgment of posterity upon the value of psychoanalysis for psychiatry, psychology, and the mental sciences in general. But I fancy that, when the history of the phase we have lived through comes to be written, German science will not have cause to be proud of those who represented it. I am not thinking of the fact that they rejected psychoanalysis or of the decisive way in which they did so; both of these things were easily intelligible, they were only to be expected and at any rate they threw no discredit upon the character of the opponents of analysis. But for the degree of arrogance which they displayed, for their conscienceless contempt of logic, and for the coarseness and bad taste of their attacks there could be no excuse. It may be said that it is childish of me to give free rein to such feelings as these now, after fifteen years have passed; nor would I do so unless I had something more to add. Years later, during the Great War, when a chorus of enemies were bringing against the German nation the charge of barbarism, a charge which sums up all that I have written above, it none the less hurt deeply to feel that my own experience would not allow me to contradict it.

One of my opponents boasted of silencing his patients as soon as they began to talk of anything sexual and evidently thought that this technique gave him a right to judge the part played by sexuality in the neuroses. Apart from emotional resistances, which were so easily explicable by the psychoanalytical theory that it was impossible to be misled by them, it seemed to me that the main obstacle to agreement lay in the fact that my opponents regarded psychoanalysis as a product of my speculative imagination and were unwilling to believe in the long, patient and unbiassed work which had gone to its making. Since in their opinion analysis had nothing to do with observation or experience, they believed that they themselves were justified in rejecting it without experience. Others again, who did not feel so strongly convinced of this, repeated in their resistance the classical manoeuvre of not looking through the microscope so as to avoid seeing what they had denied. It is remarkable, indeed, how incorrectly most people act when they are obliged to form a judgment of their own upon some new subject. I have heard for years from 'benevolent' critics— and I am told the same thing even to-day—that psychoanalysis is right up to such-and-such a point but that there it begins to exaggerate and to generalize without justification. But I know that, while nothing is more difficult than to draw such a line, the critics had been completely ignorant of the whole subject only a few weeks or days earlier.

The result of the official anathema against psychoanalysis was that the analysts began to come closer together. At the second Congress, held at Nuremberg in 1910, they formed themselves, on the proposal of Ferenczi, into an 'International Psycho-Analytical Association' divided into a number of local societies but under a common president. The Association survived the Great War and still exists, consisting to-day of branch societies in Austria, Germany, Hungary, Switzerland, Great Britain, Holland, Russia, and India, as well as two in the United States. I arranged that C. G. Jung should be appointed as the first President, which turned out later to have been a most unfortunate step. At the same time a second journal devoted to psychoanalysis was started, the *Zentralblatt für Psychoanalyse,* edited by Adler and Stekel, and a little later a third, *Imago,* edited by two non-medical analysts, H. Sachs and O. Rank, and intended to deal with the application of analysis to the mental sciences. Soon afterwards Bleuler published a paper in defence of psychoanalysis.[1] Though it was a relief to find honesty and straightforward logic for once taking part in the dispute, yet I could not feel completely satisfied by Bleuler's essay. He strove too eagerly after an appearance of impartiality; nor is it a matter of chance that it is to him that our science owes the valuable concept of *ambivalence.* In later papers Bleuler adopted such a critical attitude towards the theoretical structure of analysis and rejected or threw doubts upon such essential parts of it, that I could not help asking myself in astonishment what could be left of it for him to admire. Yet not only has he subsequently uttered the strongest pleas in favour of 'depth psychology' but he based his comprehensive study of schizophrenia upon it. Nevertheless Bleuler did not for long

---

[1]'Die Psychoanalyse Freuds', *Jahrbuch für psychoanalytische und psychopathologische Forschungen,* Bd. II., 1910.

remain a member of the International Psycho-Analytical Association; he resigned from it as a result of misunderstandings with Jung, and the Burghölzli[2] was lost to analysis.

Official disapproval could not hinder the spread of psychoanalysis either in Germany or in other countries. I have elsewhere[3] followed the stages of its growth and given the names of those who were its first representatives. In 1909 G. Stanley Hall invited Jung and me to America to go to the Clark University, Worcester, Mass., of which he was President, and to spend a week giving lectures (in German) at the celebration of the twentieth anniversary of that body's foundation. Hall was justly esteemed as a psychologist and educationalist, and had introduced psychoanalysis into his courses some years before; there was a touch of the 'king-maker' about him, a pleasure in setting up authorities and in then deposing them. We also met James J. Putnam there, the Harvard neurologist, who in spite of his age was an enthusiastic supporter of psychoanalysis and threw the whole weight of a personality that was universally respected into the defence of the cultural value of analysis and the purity of its aims. He was an estimable man, in whom, as a reaction against a predisposition to obsessional neurosis, an ethical bias predominated; and the only thing in him that we could regret was his inclination to attach psychoanalysis to a particular philosophical system and to make it the servant of moral aims. Another event of this time which made a lasting impression upon me was a meeting with William James the philosopher. I shall never forget one little scene that occurred as we were on a walk together. He stopped suddenly, handed me a bag he was carrying and asked me to walk on, saying that he would catch me up as soon as he had got

---

[2][The public mental hospital at Zurich.]
[3]'On the History of the Psycho-Analytic Movement.'

through an attack of angina pectoris which was just coming on. He died of that disease a year later; and I have always wished that I might be as fearless as he was in the face of approaching death.

At that time I was only fifty-three. I felt young and healthy, and my short visit to the new world encouraged my self-respect in every way. In Europe I felt as though I were despised; but over there I found myself received by the foremost men as an equal. As I stepped on to the platform at Worcester to deliver my *Five Lectures upon Psychoanalysis* it seemed like the realization of some incredible daydream: psychoanalysis was no longer a product of delusion, it had become a valuable part of reality. It has not lost ground in America since our visit; it is extremely popular among the lay public and is recognized by a number of official psychiatrists as an important element in medical training. Unfortunately, however, it has suffered a great deal from being watered down. Moreover, many abuses which have no relation to it find a cover under its name, and there are few opportunities for any thorough training in technique or theory. In America, too, it has come in conflict with Behaviourism, a theory which is naïve enough to boast that it has put the whole problem of psychology completely out of court.

In Europe during the years 1911–13 two secessionist movements from psychoanalysis took place, led by men who had previously played a considerable part in the young science, Alfred Adler and C. G. Jung. Both movements seemed most threatening and quickly obtained a large following. But their strength lay, not in their own content, but in the temptation which they offered of being freed from what were felt as the repellent findings of psychoanalysis without the necessity of rejecting its actual material. Jung attempted to give to the facts of analysis a fresh interpretation of an abstract, impersonal and non-historical character, and thus hoped to escape the need for recognizing the importance of infantile sexuality and of the Oedipus complex as well as the necessity for any analysis of childhood. Adler seemed to depart still further from psychoanalysis; he entirely repudiated the importance of sexuality, traced back the formation both of character and of the neuroses solely to men's desire for power and to their need to compensate for their constitutional inferiority, and threw all the psychological discoveries of psychoanalysis to the winds. But what he had rejected forced its way back into his closed system under other names; his 'masculine protest' is nothing else than repression unjustifiably sexualized. The criticism with which the two heretics were met was a mild one; I only insisted that both Adler and Jung should cease to describe their theories as 'psychoanalysis'. After a lapse of ten years it can be asserted that both of these attempts against psychoanalysis have blown over without doing any harm.

If a community is based upon agreement upon a few cardinal points, it is obvious that people who have abandoned that common ground will cease to belong to it. Yet the secession of former pupils has often been brought up against me as a sign of my intolerance or has been regarded as evidence of some special fatality that hangs over me. It is a sufficient answer to point out that in contrast to those who have left me, like Jung, Adler, Stekel, and a few besides, there are a great number of men, like Abraham, Eitingon, Ferenczi, Rank, Jones, Brill, Sachs, Pfister, van Emden, Reik, and others, who have worked with me for some fifteen years in loyal collaboration and for the most part in uninterrupted friendship. I have only mentioned the oldest of my pupils, who have already made a distinguished name for themselves in the literature of psychoanalysis; if I have passed over others, that is not to be taken as a slight, and indeed among those who are young and have joined me lately talents are to be found on which great hopes may be set. But I think I can say in my defence that an intolerant man, dominated by an arrogant belief in his own infallibility, would never have been able to maintain his hold upon so large a number of intelligent people, especially if he had at his command as few practical attractions as I had.

The Great War, which broke up so many other organizations, could do nothing against our 'International'. The first meeting after the war took place in 1920, at The Hague, on neutral ground. It was moving to see how hospitably the Dutch welcomed the starving and impoverished subjects of the Central European states; and I believe this was the first occasion in a ruined world on which Englishmen and Germans sat at the same table for the friendly discussion of scientific interests. Both in Germany and in the countries of Western Europe the war had actually stimulated interest in psychoanalysis. The observation of war neuroses had at last opened the eyes of the medical profession to the importance of psychogenesis in neurotic disturbances, and some of our psychological conceptions, such as the 'advantage of being ill' and the 'flight into illness', suddenly became popular. The last Congress before the German collapse, which was held at Budapest in 1918, was attended by official representatives of the allied governments of the Central European powers, and they agreed to the establishment of psychoanalytic stations for the treatment of war neuroses. But this point was never reached. Similarly too the comprehensive plans made by one of our leading members, Dr. Anton von Freund, for establishing in Budapest a centre for analytic study and treatment came to grief as a result of the political disorders of the time and of the premature death of their generous author. At a later date some of his ideas were put into execution by Max Eitingon, who in 1920 founded a psychoanalytical clinic in Berlin. During the brief period of Bolshevist rule in Hungary, Ferenczi was able to carry on a successful course of instruction as the official representative of psychoanalysis at the University of Budapest. After the war our opponents announced with great joy that events had produced a conclusive argument against the validity of the theses of analysis. The war neuroses, they said, had proved that sexual factors were unnecessary to the aetiology of neurotic disorders. But their triumph was frivolous and premature. For on the one hand no one had been able to carry out a thorough analysis of a case of war neurosis, so that in fact nothing whatever was known for certain as to their motivation and no conclusions could be drawn from this uncertainty. While on the other hand psychoanalysis had long before arrived at the concept of narcissism and of narcissistic neuroses, in which the subject's libido is attached to his own ego instead of to an object. Though on other occasions, therefore, the charge was brought against psychoanalysis of having made an unjustifiable extension of the concept of sexuality, yet, when it became convenient for polemical ends, this crime was forgotten and we were once more held down to the narrowest meaning of the word.

If the preliminary cathartic period is left on one side, the history of psychoanalysis falls from my point of view into two phases. In the first of these I stood alone and had to do all the work myself: this was from 1895–96 until 1906 or 1907. In the second phase, lasting from then until the present time, the contributions of my pupils and collaborators have been growing more and more in importance, so that to-day, when a grave illness warns me of the approaching end, I can think with a quiet mind of the cessation of my own labours. For that very reason, however, it is impossible for me in this *Autobiographical Study* to deal as fully with the progress of psychoanalysis during the second phase as I did with its gradual rise during the first phase, which was concerned with my own activity alone. I feel that I should only be justified in mentioning here those new discoveries in which I still played a prominent part, in particular, therefore, those made in the sphere of narcissism, of the theory of the instincts, and of the application of psychoanalysis to the psychoses.

I must begin by adding that increasing experience showed more and more plainly that the Oedipus complex was the nucleus of the neurosis. It was at once the climax of infantile sexual life and the point of junction from which all of its later developments proceeded. But if so, it was no longer possible to expect analysis to discover a factor that was specific in the aetiology of the neuroses. It must be true, as Jung expressed it so well in the early days when he was still an analyst, that neuroses have no peculiar content which belongs exclusively to them but that neurotics break down at the same difficulties that are successfully overcome by normal people. This discovery was very far from being a disappointment. It was in complete harmony with another one: that the depth-psychology revealed by psychoanalysis was in fact the psychology of the normal mind. Our path had been like that of chemistry: the great qualitative differences between substances were traced back to quantitative variations in the proportions in which the same elements were combined.

In the Oedipus complex the libido was attached to the image of the parents. But earlier there was a period in which there were no such objects. There followed from this fact the concept (of fundamental importance for the libido theory) of a state in which the subject's libido filled his own ego and had that for its object. This state could be called *narcissism* or self-love. A moment's reflection showed that this state never completely ceases. All through the subject's life his ego remains the great reservoir of his libido, from which the attachments to objects (the *object-cathexes*) radiate out and into which the libido can stream back again from the objects. Thus narcissistic libido is constantly being converted into object-libido, and *vice versa*. An excellent instance of the length to which this conversion can go is afforded by the sexual or sublimated devotion which involves a sacrifice of the self. Whereas hitherto in considering the process of repression attention had only been paid to what was repressed, these ideas made it also possible to form a correct estimate of the repressing forces. It had been said that repression was set in action by the instincts of self-preservation operating in the ego (the *ego-instincts*) and that it was brought to bear upon the libidinal instincts. But since the instincts of self-preservation were now recognized as also being of a libidinal nature, as being narcissistic libido, the process of repression was seen to be a process occurring within the libido itself; narcissistic libido was opposed to object-libido, the interests of self-preservation defended themselves against the demands of object-love, that is, against the demands of sexuality in the narrower sense.

There is no more urgent need in psychology than for a securely founded theory of the instincts on which it might then be possible to build further. Nothing of the sort exists, however, and psychoanalysis is driven to making tentative efforts towards some such theory. It began by drawing a contrast between the ego-instincts (the instinct of self-preservation, hunger) and the libidinal instincts (love), but later replaced it by a new contrast between narcissistic and object-libido. This was clearly not the last word on the subject;

biological considerations seemed to make it impossible to remain content with assuming the existence of only a single class of instincts.

In the work of my later years (*Beyond the Pleasure Principle, Group Psychology and the Analysis of the Ego,* and *The Ego and the Id,*)[4] I have given free rein to the inclination which I kept down for so long to speculation and I have also taken stock of a new solution of the problem of the instincts. I have combined the instincts for self-preservation and for the preservation of the species under the concept of *Eros* and have contrasted with it an instinct of death or destruction which works in silence. Instinct in general is regarded as a kind of elasticity of living things, an impulsion towards the restoration of a situation which once existed but was brought to an end by some external disturbance. This essentially conservative character of instincts is exemplified by the phenomena of the *compulsion to repeat.* The picture which life presents to us is the result of the working of Eros and the death-instinct together and against each other.

It remains to be seen whether this construction will turn out to be serviceable. Although it arose from a desire to fix some of the most important theoretical ideas of psychoanalysis, it goes far beyond psychoanalysis. I have repeatedly heard it said contemptuously that it is impossible to take a science seriously whose most general concepts are as lacking in precision as those of libido and of instinct in psychoanalysis. But this reproach is based upon a complete misconception of the facts. Clear fundamental concepts and sharply drawn definitions are only possible in the mental sciences in so far as the latter seek to fit a department of facts into the

---

[4][Jenseits des Lustprinzips, Vienna, 1920, *Massenpsychologie und Ichanalyse.* Vienna, 1921, and *Das Ich und das Es,* Vienna, 1923.]

frame of a logical system. In the natural sciences, of which
psychology is one, such clear-cut general concepts are super-
fluous and indeed impossible. Zoology and Botany did not
start from correct and adequate definitions of an animal and
a plant; to this very day biology has been unable to give any
certain meaning to the concept of life. Physics itself, indeed,
would never have made any advance if it had had to wait
until its concepts of matter, force, gravitation, and so on,
had reached the desirable degree of clarity and precision.
The fundamental concepts or most general ideas in any of
the disciplines of science are always left indeterminate at
first and are only explained to begin with by reference to the
realm of phenomena from which they were derived; it is
only by means of a progressive analysis of the material of
observation that they can be made clear and can find a
significant and consistent meaning. I have always felt it as
a gross injustice that people always refused to treat psychoanalysis like any other science. This refusal found an expression in the raising of the most obstinate objections. Psychoanalysis was constantly reproached for its incompletenesses
and insufficiencies; though it is plain that a science based
upon observation has no alternative but to work out its
findings piecemeal and to solve its problems step by step.
Again, when I endeavoured to obtain for the sexual function
the recognition which had so long been withheld from it,
psychoanalytic theory was branded as 'pan-sexualism'. And
when I laid stress upon the hitherto neglected importance
of the part played by the accidental impressions of early
youth, I was told that psychoanalysis was denying constitutional and hereditary factors—a thing which I had never
dreamt of doing. It was a case of contradiction at any price
and by any methods.

I had already made attempts at earlier stages of my work

to arrive at some more general points of view, starting from the observations of psychoanalysis. In a short essay, 'Formulations regarding the Two Principles of Mental Functioning',[5] published in 1911, I drew attention (and there was, of course, nothing original in this) to the domination of the *pleasure-pain principle* in mental life and to its displacement by the so-called *reality principle*. Later on (1915–17) I made an attempt to produce a 'Metapsychology'. By this I meant a method of approach according to which every mental process is considered in relation to three co-ordinates, which I described as *dynamic, topographical,* and *economic* respectively; and this seemed to me to represent the furthest goal that psychology could attain. The attempt remained no more than a torso; after writing two or three papers—'Instincts and their Vicissitudes', 'Repression', 'The Unconscious', 'Mourning and Melancholia', etc.[6]—I broke off, wisely perhaps, since the time for theoretical predications of this kind had not yet come. In my latest speculative works I have set about the task of dissecting our mental apparatus on the basis of the analytic view of pathological facts and have divided it into an *ego,* an *id,* and a *super-ego.*[7] The super-ego is the heir of the Oedipus complex and represents the ethical standards of mankind.

I should not like to create an impression that during this last period of my work I have turned my back upon patient observation and have abandoned myself entirely to speculation. I have on the contrary always remained in the closest touch with the analytic material and have never ceased working at detailed points of clinical or technical impor-

---

[5][*Jahrbuch für psychoanalytische und psychopathologische Forschungen,* Bd. III, 1911 English translation in Freud's *Collected Papers,* vol. iv.]
[6][Published in the *Zeitschrift für Psychoanalyse* between 1915 and 1917. English translation in Freud's *Collected Papers,* vol. iv.]
[7]*The Ego and the Id.*

tance. Even when I have moved away from observation, I have carefully avoided any contact with philosophy proper. This avoidance has been greatly facilitated by constitutional incapacity. I was always open to the ideas of G. T. Fechner and have followed that thinker upon many important points. The large extent to which psychoanalysis coincides with the philosophy of Schopenhauer—not only did he assert the dominance of the emotions and the supreme importance of sexuality but he was even aware of the mechanism of repression—is not to be traced to my acquaintance with his teaching. I read Schopenhauer very late in my life. Nietzsche, another philosopher whose guesses and intuitions often agree in the most astonishing way with the laborious findings of psychoanalysis, was for a long time avoided by me on that very account; I was less concerned with the question of priority than with keeping my mind unembarrassed.

The neuroses were the first subject of analysis, and for a long time they were the only one. No analyst could doubt that medical practice was wrong in separating those disorders from the psychoses and in attaching them to the organic nervous diseases. The theory of the neuroses belongs to psychiatry and is indispensable as an introduction to it. It would seem, however, that the analytical study of the psychoses is impracticable owing to its lack of therapeutic results. Mental patients are as a rule without the capacity for forming a positive transference, so that the principle instrument of analytic technique is inapplicable to them. There are nevertheless a number of methods of approach to be found. Transference is often not so completely absent but that it can be used to a certain extent; and analysis has achieved undoubted successes with cyclical depressions, light paranoic modifications, and partial schizophrenias. It has at least been a benefit to science that in many cases the diagnosis can oscillate for quite a long time between assum-

ing the presence of a psycho-neurosis or of a dementia praecox; for therapeutic attempts initiated in such cases have
resulted in valuable discoveries before they have had to be
broken off. But the chief consideration in this connection is
that so many things that in the neuroses have to be labori-
ously fetched up from the depths are found in the psychoses
upon the surface, visible to every eye. So that the best
subjects for the demonstration of many of the assertions of
analysis are provided by the psychiatric clinic. It was thus
bound to happen before long that analysis would find its way
to the objects of psychiatric observation. At a very early date
(1896) I was able to establish in a case of paranoid dementia
the presence of the same aetiological factors and the same
emotional complexes as in the neuroses. Jung explained
some most puzzling stereotypies in dements by bringing
them into relation with the patients' life-histories; Bleuler
demonstrated the existence in various psychoses of mechanisms like those which analysis had discovered in neurotics.
Since then analysts have never relaxed their efforts to come
to an understanding of the psychoses. Especially since it has
been possible to work with the concept of narcissism, they
have managed, now in this place and now in that, to get a
glimpse beyond the wall. Most of all, no doubt, was achieved
by Abraham in his elucidation of melancholia. It is true that
in this sphere all our knowledge is not yet converted into
therapeutic power; but the mere theoretical gain is not to
be despised, and we may be content to wait for its practical
application. In the long run even the psychiatrists have been
unable to resist the convincing force of their own clinical
material. At the present time German psychiatry is under-
going a kind of 'peaceful penetration' by analytic views.
While they continually declare that they will never be psychoanalysts, that they do not belong to the 'orthodox' school
or agree with its exaggerations, and in particular that they

do not believe in the predominance of the sexual factor, nevertheless the majority of the younger workers take over one piece or another of analytical theory and apply it in their own fashion to the material. All the signs point to the proximity of further developments in the same direction.

VI

I now watch from a distance the symptomatic reactions that are accompanying the introduction of psychoanalysis into the France which was for so long refractory. It seems like a reproduction of something I have lived through before, and yet it has peculiarities of its own. Objections of incredible simplicity are raised, such as that French sensitiveness is offended by the pedantry and crudity of psychoanalytical terminology. (One cannot help being reminded of Lessing's immortal Chevalier Riccaut de la Marlinière.[1]) Another comment has a more serious ring (a Professor of Psychology at the Sorbonne did not think it beneath him): the whole method of thought of psychoanalysis is inconsistent with the *génie latin*. Here the Anglo-Saxon allies of France, who count as supporters of analysis, are explicitly thrown over. Anyone hearing the remark would suppose that psychoanalysis had been the favourite child of the *génie teutonique* and had been clasped to its heart from the moment of birth.

---

[1][The comic French soldier of fortune in *Minna von Barnhelm* who is amazed when his sharp practice at cards is described as cheating: 'Comment Mademoiselle? Vous appelez cela "cheating"? Corriger la fortune, l'enchaîner sous ses doigts, être sûr de son fait—do the Germans call that "cheating"? Cheating! Oh, what a poor language, what a crude language German must be!']

In France the interest in psychoanalysis began among the men of letters. To understand this, it must be borne in mind that from the time of the writing of *The Interpretation of Dreams* psychoanalysis ceased to be a purely medical subject. Between its appearance in Germany and in France lies the history of its numerous applications to departments of literature and of aesthetics, to the history of religions and to pre-history, to mythology, to folk-lore, to education, and so on. None of these things have much to do with medicine; in fact it is only through psychoanalysis that they are connected with it. I have no business, therefore, to go into them in detail in these pages.[2] I cannot pass them over completely in silence, however, for on the one hand they are essential to a correct appreciation of the nature and value of psychoanalysis, and on the other hand I have, after all, undertaken to give an account of my life-work. The beginnings of the majority of these applications of psychoanalysis will be found in my works. Here and there I have gone a little way along the path in order to gratify my non-medical interests. Later on, others (not only doctors, but specialists in the various fields as well) have followed in my tracks and penetrated far into the different subjects. But since my programme limits me to a mention of my own share in these applications of psychoanalysis, I can only give a quite inadequate picture of their extent and importance.

A number of suggestions came to me out of the Oedipus complex, the ubiquity of which gradually dawned on me. The poet's choice, or his invention, of such a terrible subject seemed puzzling; and so too did the overwhelming effect of its dramatic treatment, and the general nature of such tragedies of destiny. But all of this became intelligible when one

---

[2][The present work, it will be remembered, originally formed part of a series of medical autobiographies.]

realized that a universal law of mental life had here been captured in all its emotional significance. Fate and the oracle were no more than materializations of an internal necessity; and the fact of the hero sinning without his knowledge and against his intentions was evidently a right expression of the *unconscious* nature of his criminal tendencies. From understanding this tragedy of destiny it was only a step further to understanding a tragedy of character—*Hamlet*, which had been admired for three hundred years without its meaning being discovered or its author's motives guessed. It could scarcely be a chance that this neurotic creation of the poet should have broken down, like his numberless fellows in the real world, at the Oedipus complex; for Hamlet was faced with the task of taking vengeance upon another for the two deeds which are the subject of the Oedipus desires, and before that task his arm was paralysed by his own obscure sense of guilt. Shakespeare wrote *Hamlet* very soon after his father's death.[3] The suggestions made by me for the analysis of this tragedy were fully worked out later on by Ernest Jones. And the same example was afterwards used by Otto Rank as the starting-point for his investigation of the choice of material made by dramatists. In his large volume upon the incest theme[4] he was able to show how often imaginative writers have taken as their subject the themes of the Oedipus situation, and traced in the different literatures of the world the way in which the material has been transformed, modified, and softened.

It was tempting to go on from there to an attempt at an analysis of poetic and artistic creation in general. The realm of imagination was evidently a 'sanctuary' made during the

---

[3](Additional note, 1935.) I have particular reasons for no longer wishing to lay any emphasis upon this point.
[4]*Das Inzest-Motiv in Dichtung und Sage*, Vienna, 1912.

painful transition from the pleasure principle to the reality principle in order to provide a substitute for the gratification of instincts which had to be given up in real life. The artist, like the neurotic, had withdrawn from an unsatisfying reality into this world of imagination; but, unlike the neurotic, he knew how to find a way back from it and once more to get a firm foothold in reality. His creations, works of art, were the imaginary gratifications of unconscious wishes, just as dreams are; and like them they were in the nature of compromises, since they too were forced to avoid any open conflict with the forces of repression. But they differed from the asocial, narcissistic products of dreaming in that they were calculated to arouse interest in other people and were able to evoke and to gratify the same unconscious wishes in them too. Besides this, they made use of the perceptual pleasure of formal beauty as what I have called an 'incitement-premium'. What psychoanalysis was able to do was to take the inter-relations between the impressions of the artist's life, his chance experiences, and his works, and from them to construct his constitution and the impulses at work in it—that is to say, that part of him which he shared with all men. With this aim in view, for instance, I made Leonardo da Vinci the subject of a study, which is based upon a single memory of childhood related by him and which aims chiefly at explaining his picture of 'St. Anne with the Virgin and Child'. It does not appear that the enjoyment of a work of art is spoiled by the knowledge gained from such an analysis. The layman may perhaps expect too much from analysis in this respect, for it must be admitted that it throws no light upon the two problems which probably interest him the most. It can do nothing towards elucidating the nature of the artistic gift, nor can it explain the means by which the artist works—artistic technique.

I was able to show from a short story by W. Jensen called

Gradiva, which has no particular merit in itself, that invented dreams can be interpreted in the same way as real ones and that the unconscious mechanisms familiar to us in the 'dream-work' are thus also operative in the processes of imaginative writing. My book upon *Wit and its Relation to the Unconscious*[5] was a side-issue indirectly derived from *The Interpretation of Dreams.* The only friend of mine who was at that time interested in my work remarked to me that my interpretations of dreams often impressed him as being like jokes. In order to throw some light on this impression, I began to investigate jokes and found that their essence lay in the technical methods employed in them, and that these were the same as the means used in the 'dream-work'—that is to say, condensation, displacement, the representation of a thing by its opposite or by a triviality, and so on. This led to an economic enquiry as to the origin of the high degree of pleasure obtained from hearing a joke. And to this the answer was that it was due to the momentary suspension of the energy expended upon maintaining repression owing to the attraction exercised by the offer of a premium of pleasure *(fore-pleasure.)*

I myself set a higher value upon my contributions to the psychology of religion, which began in 1907 with the establishment of a remarkable similarity between obsessive acts and religious practices or ritual. Without as yet understanding the deeper connections, I described the obsessional neurosis as a distorted private religion and religion as a kind of universal obsessional neurosis. Later on, in 1912, the explicit indications of Jung as to the far-reaching analogies between the mental products of neurotics and of primitive peoples led me to turn my attention to that subject. In four essays,

---

[5][First German edition, under the title of *Der Witz und seine Beziehung zum Unbewussten,* Vienna, 1905]

which were collected into a book with the title of *Totem and Taboo*, [6] I showed that the dread of incest was even more marked among primitive than among civilized races and had given rise to very special measures of defence against it; I examined the relations between taboo-prohibitions (the earliest form in which moral restrictions make their appearance) and emotional ambivalence; and I discovered under the primitive scheme of the universe known as animism the principle of the overestimation of the importance of psychical reality, the principle of 'the omnipotence of thoughts', which also lies at the root of magic. I developed the comparison with the obsessional neurosis at every point, and showed how many of the postulates of primitive mental life are still in force in that remarkable disorder. Above all, however, I was attracted by totemism, the first system of organization in primitive tribes, a system in which the beginnings of social order are united with a rudimentary religion and the implacable domination of a small number of taboo-prohibitions. The being that is honoured is ultimately always an animal, from which the clan also claims to be descended. Many indications pointed to the conclusion that every race, even the most highly developed, had once passed through the stage of totemism.

The chief literary sources of my studies in this field were the well-known works of J. G. Frazer (*Totemism and Exogamy* and *The Golden Bough*), a mine of valuable facts and opinions. But Frazer effected little towards elucidating the problems of totemism; he had several times fundamentally altered his views on the subject, and the other ethnologists and pre-historians seemed in equal uncertainty and disagreement. My starting-point was the striking correspondence between the two taboo-injunctions of totemism (not to kill

---

[6][First German edition, under the title of *Totem and Tabu*, Vienna, 1913.]

the totem and not to have sexual relations with any woman of the same totem-clan) and the two elements of the Oedipus complex (killing the father and taking the mother to wife). I was therefore tempted to equate the totem-animal with the father; and in fact primitive peoples themselves do this explicitly, by honouring it as the fore-father of the clan. There next came to my help two facts from psychoanalysis, a lucky observation of a child made by Ferenczi, which made it possible to speak of an 'infantile return of totemism', and the analysis of early animal-phobias in children, which so often showed that the animal was a substitute for the father, a substitute on to which the fear of the father derived from the Oedipus complex had been displaced. Not much was lacking to enable me to recognize the killing of the father as the nucleus of totemism and the starting-point in the formation of religion.

This missing element was supplied when I became acquainted with W. Robertson Smith's work, *The Religion of the Semites.* Its author (a man of genius who was both a physicist and a biblical expert) introduced the so-called totem-feast as an essential part of the totemistic religion. Once a year the totem animal, which was at other times regarded as sacred, was solemnly killed in the presence of all the members of the clan, was devoured and was then mourned over. The mourning was followed by a great festival. When I further took into account Darwin's conjecture that men originally lived in hordes, each under the domination of a single powerful, violent and jealous male, there rose before me out of all these components the following hypothesis, or, I would rather say, vision. The father of the primal horde, since he was an unlimited despot, had seized all the women for himself; his sons, being dangerous to him as rivals, had been killed or driven away. One day, however, the sons came together and united to overwhelm, kill, and devour their father, who had been their enemy but also their ideal. After the deed they were unable to take over their heritage since they stood in one another's way. Under the influence of failure and regret they learned to come to an agreement among themselves, they banded themselves into a clan of brothers by the help of the ordinances of totemism, which aimed at preventing a repetition of such a deed, and they jointly undertook to forego the possession of the women on whose account they had killed their father. They were then driven to finding strange women, and this was the origin of the exogamy which is so closely bound up with totemism. The totem-feast was the commemoration of the fearful deed from which sprang man's sense of guilt (or 'original sin') and which was the beginning at once of social organization, of religion and of ethical restrictions.

Now whether we suppose that such a possibility was a historical event or not, it brings the formation of religion within the circle of the father-complex and bases it upon the ambivalence which dominates that complex. After the totem animal had ceased to serve as a substitute for him, the primal father, at once feared and hated, honoured and envied, became the prototype of God himself. The son's rebelliousness and his affection for his father struggled against each other through a constant succession of compromises, which sought on the one hand to atone for the act of parricide and on the other to consolidate the advantages it had brought. This view of religion throws a particularly clear light upon the psychological basis of Christianity, in which, it may be added, the ceremony of the totem-feast still survives with but little distortion in the form of Communion. I should like explicitly to mention that this last observation was not made by me but is to be found in the works of Robertson Smith and Frazer.

Theodor Reik and G. Róheim, the ethnologist, have

taken up the line of thought which I developed in *Totem and Taboo* and, in a series of important works, have extended it, amplified it, or corrected it. I myself have since returned to it more than once, in the course of my investigations into the 'unconscious sense of guilt' (which also plays such an important part among the motives of neurotic suffering) and in my attempts at forming a closer connection between social psychology and the psychology of the individual.[7] I have moreover made use of the idea of an archaic inheritance from the 'primal horde' epoch of mankind's development in explaining susceptibility to hypnosis.

I have taken but little direct part in certain other applications of psychoanalysis, though they are none the less of general interest. It is only a step from the phantasies of individual neurotics to the imaginative creations of groups and peoples as we find them in myths, legends, and fairy tales. Mythology became the special province of Otto Rank; the interpretation of myths, the tracing of them back to the familiar unconscious complexes of infancy, the replacing of astral explanations by a discovery of human motives, all of this is to a large extent due to his analytic efforts. The subject of symbolism has also found many students among my followers. Symbolism has brought psychoanalysis many enemies; many enquirers with unduly prosaic minds have never been able to forgive it the recognition of symbolism, which followed from the interpretation of dreams. But analysis is guiltless of the discovery of symbolism, for it had long been known in other regions of thought (such as folk-lore, legends, and myths) and plays an even larger part in them than in the 'language of dreams'.

I myself have contributed nothing to the application of analysis to education. It was natural, however, that the ana-

---

[7] *The Ego and the Id* and *Group Psychology and the Analysis of the Ego.*

lytic discoveries as to the sexual life and mental development of children should attract the attention of educators and make them see their problems in a new light. Dr. Oskar Pfister, a protestant pastor at Zurich, led the way as a tireless pioneer along these lines, nor did he find the practice of analysis incompatible with the retention of his religion, though it is true that this was of a sublimated kind. Among the many others who worked alongside of him I may mention Frau Dr. Hug-Hellmuth and Dr. S. Bernfeld, both of Vienna.[8] The application of analysis to the prophylactic education of healthy children and to the correcting of those who, though not actually neurotic, have deviated from the normal course of development has led to one consequence which is of practical importance. It is no longer possible to restrict the practice of psychoanalysis to physicians and to exclude laymen from it. In fact,. a physician who has not been through a special training is, in spite of his diploma, a layman in analysis, and a non-physician who has been suitably trained can, with occasional reference to a physician, carry out the analytic treatment not only of children but also of neurotics.

By a process of development against which it would have been useless to struggle, the word 'psychoanalysis' has itself become ambiguous. While it was originally the name of a particular therapeutic method, it has now also become the name of a science—the science of unconscious mental processes. By itself this science is seldom able to deal with a problem completely, but it seems destined to give valuable contributory help in a large number of regions of knowledge. The sphere of application of psychoanalysis extends as far as

---

[8](Additional note, 1935:) Since these words were written child analysis in particular has gained a powerful momentum owing to the work of Mrs. Melanie Klein and of my daughter Anna Freud.

that of psychology, to which it forms a complement of the greatest moment.

Looking back, then, over the patchwork of my life's labours, I can say that I have made many beginnings and thrown out many suggestions. Something will come of them in the future, though I cannot myself tell whether it will be much or little. I can, however, express a hope that I have opened up a pathway for an important advance in our knowledge.

POSTSCRIPT (1935)

The editor of this series of autobiographical studies did not, so far as I know, consider the possibility that after a certain lapse of time a sequel might be written to any of them; and it may be that such an event has occurred only in the present instance. I am undertaking the task since my American publisher desires to issue the little work in a new edition. It first appeared in America in 1927 (published by Brentano) under the title of *An Autobiographical Study,* but it was injudiciously brought out in the same volume as another essay of mine which gave its title, *The Problem of Lay-Analyses,* to the whole book and so obscured the present work.

Two themes run through these pages: the story of my life and the history of psychoanalysis. They are intimately interwoven. This *Autobiographical Study* shows how psychoanalysis came to be the whole content of my life and rightly assumes that no personal experiences of mine are of any interest in comparison to my relations with that science.

Shortly before I wrote this study it seemed as though my life would soon be brought to an end by the recurrence of a malignant disease; but surgical skill saved me in 1923 and I was able to continue my life and my work, though no longer in freedom from pain. In the period of more than ten years that has passed since then, I have never ceased my analytic work nor my writing—as is proved by the completion of the twelfth volume of the German edition of my collected works. But I myself find that a significant change has come about. Threads which in the course of my development had become intertangled have now begun to separate; interests which I had acquired in the later part of my life have receded, while the older and original ones become prominent once more. It is true that in this last decade I have carried out some important pieces of analytic work, such as the revision of the problem of anxiety in my book *Hemmung, Symptom and Angst* (published in 1926) or the simple explanation of sexual 'fetishism' which I was able to make in 1927. Nevertheless it would be true to say that, since I put forward my hypothesis of the existence of two kinds of instinct (Eros and the death instinct) and since I proposed a division of the mental personality into an ego, a super-ego, and an id (in 1923), I have made no further decisive contributions to psychoanalysis: what I have written on the subject since then has been either unessential or would soon have been supplied by someone else. This circumstance is connected with an alteration in myself, with what might be described as a phase of regressive development. My interest, after making a lifelong *détour* through the natural sciences, medicine and psychotherapy, returned to the cultural problems which had fascinated me long before, when I was a youth scarcely old enough for thinking. At the very climax of my psychoanalytic work, in 1912, I had already attempted in *Totem and Taboo* to make use of the newly discovered findings of analysis in order to investigate the origins of religion and morality. I now carried this work a stage further in two later essays, *The Future of an Illusion* (1927) and *Civilization and its Discontents* (1930). I perceived ever more clearly that the events of human history, the interactions between human nature, cultural development and the precipitates of primaeval experiences (the most prominent example of which is religion) are no more than a reflection of the dynamic conflicts between the ego, the id, and the super-ego, which psychoanalysis studies in the individual—are the very same processes repeated upon a wider stage. In *The Future of an Illusion* I expressed an essentially negative valuation of religion. Later, I found a formula which did better justice to it: while granting that its power lies in the truth which it contains, I showed that that truth was not a material but a historical truth.

These studies, which, though they originate in psychoanalysis, stretch far beyond it, have perhaps awakened more public sympathy than psychoanalysis itself. They may have played a part in creating the short-lived illusion that I was among the writers to whom a great nation like Germany was ready to listen. It was in 1929 that, with words no less pregnant than friendly, Thomas Mann, one of the acknowledged spokesmen of the German people, found a place for me in the history of modern thought. A little later my daughter Anna, acting as my proxy, was given a civic reception in the Rathaus at Frankfort-on-Main on the occasion of my being awarded the Goethe Prize for 1930. This was the climax of my life as a citizen. Soon afterwards the boundaries of our country narrowed and the nation would know no more of us.

And here I may be allowed to break off these autobiographical notes. The public has no claim to learn any more of my personal affairs—of my struggles, my disappointments, and my successes. I have in any case been more open and frank in some of my writings (such as *The Interpretation of Dreams* and *The Psychopathology of Everyday Life*) than people usually are who describe their lives for their contemporaries or for posterity. I have had small thanks for it, and from my experience I cannot recommend anyone to follow my example.

I must add a few more words upon the history of psycho-analysis during the last decade. There can no longer be any doubt that it will continue; it has proved its capacity to survive and to develop both as a branch of knowledge and as a therapeutic method. The number of its supporters (organized into the International Psycho-Analytical Association) has considerably increased. In addition to the older local groups (in Vienna, Berlin, Budapest, London, Holland, Switzerland, and Russia), societies have since been formed in Paris and Calcutta, two in Japan, several in the United States, and quite recently one each in Jerusalem and South Africa and two in Scandinavia. Out of their own funds these local societies support (or are in process of forming) training institutes, in which instruction in the practice of psycho-analysis is given according to a uniform plan, and out-patient clinics in which experienced analysts as well as students give free treatment to patients of limited means. Every other year the members of the International Psycho-Analytical Association hold a Congress at which scientific papers are read and questions of organization decided. The thirteenth of these congresses (which I myself can no longer attend) took place at Lucerne in 1934. From a core of interests that are common to all members of the Association, their work radiates in many different directions. Some lay most stress upon clarifying and deepening our knowledge of psychology, while others are concerned with keeping in contact with medicine and psychiatry. From the practical point of view, some analysts have set themselves the task of bringing about the recognition of psychoanalysis at the universities and its inclusion in the medical curriculum, whereas others are content to remain outside these institutions and maintain that psychoanalysis is no less important in the field of education than in that of medicine. It happens from time to time that an analytic worker may find himself isolated in an attempt to emphasize some single one of the findings or views of psychoanalysis at the expense of all the rest. Nevertheless, the whole impression is a satisfactory one—of serious scientific work carried on at a high level.

INDEX